James Campbell, an a
historian, is Seear Fell
and History of Art at
Cambridge. His books
A World History and *Bri*
both published by Tha

JAMES W. P. CAMPBELL

BUILDING ST PAUL'S

With 52 illustrations

For my goddaughter, Lucy

Acknowledgments

Many of the ideas in this book have grown out of discussions I have had with others. While their contributions have been invaluable, I must stress that any mistakes that have crept in are entirely my own. I would particularly like to thank Timothy Kent FSA (through whose support I was given a Fellowship of the Society of Antiquaries); Dr Norma Aubertin Potter and the staff of the Codrington Library, All Souls, Oxford; Adrian James and the staff of the Society of Antiquaries; Maddie Brown and the staff of the library of the Faculty of Architecture and History of Art, University of Cambridge; the staff of the Guildhall Library Archives and Drawing Collection; Jo Wisdom, librarian, Chris Faunch, archivist, and Emma Hardisty of St Paul's; Martin Stancliffe, Surveyor to the Fabric; Robert Bowles, engineer; Dr Gordon Higgott; Dr Anthony Geraghty; and Will Pryce, who took many new photographs. Most of all, I would like to thank my wife, Maisie, and my son, Hamish, who have been so very patient while I have been engaged in completing this book.

On the cover: Wren's pre-Fire design for adding a dome
to the old St Paul's (see p. 22). Courtesy the Warden and
Fellows of All Souls College, Oxford (AS II, 7)

First published in the United Kingdom in 2007 by
Thames & Hudson Ltd, 181A High Holborn,
London WC1V 7QX

This compact paperback edition published in 2020

Building St Paul's © 2007 and 2020 James Campbell

British Library Cataloguing-in-Publication Data
A catalogue record for this book is available
from the British Library

ISBN 978-0-500-29550-2

Printed and bound in the UK by CPI (UK) Ltd

To find out about all our publications, please visit
www.thamesandhudson.com. There you can subscribe
to our e-newsletter, browse or download our current
catalogue, and buy any titles that are in print.

CONTENTS

PREFACE

This short book is written for all those who have ever stood in St Paul's Cathedral, looked up in awe, and wondered how anyone managed to create such a building. It tells the story of how this great edifice was constructed. St Paul's Cathedral is one of the few great cathedrals designed and overseen by a single person and completed in their lifetime. However, as this book shows, its design and construction were more complicated than this suggests.

By following the process from beginning to end, it is possible to understand not only how such a building was erected in the seventeenth century, but also a great deal about how we build today. There are, of course, some obvious differences in lifting technology and scaffolding; and the use of steel and concrete has taken over from masonry and brick for the construction of large buildings; and pirates do not normally steal the building materials today. In other matters surprisingly little has changed. The same concerns about design integrity, functionality, structural stability, strikes, delegation, corruption, bribery, profiteering and material supply remain.

The story of St Paul's provides us with a window into daily life in seventeenth-century London. It was built at a time of profound change. Many of those involved in its construction were key players in both politics and in the scientific revolution that dominated the period. It also tells us about the lives of the ordinary workers who laboured on the cathedral in the sun and rain, wind and snow.

What makes St Paul's particularly interesting is the richness of the sources that exist for this extraordinary building, which is one of the best-documented in history. As well as nearly 300 original architectural drawings, a substantial documentary archive survives. To try to prevent corruption, those involved in the construction were required to keep meticulous audited records of every penny spent throughout the works. Over a hundred books of accounts, contracts, logbooks and registers have been preserved, along with a large number of boxes filled with receipts, bills, letters and notes. Collectively these allow us to recreate a vivid picture of what life was like on a building site in the seventeenth century and provide a detailed account of how the cathedral was built. They force us to look anew at the most important source of all: the building itself. St Paul's is full of clues to its construction, and despite its relatively simple appearance it is, as we shall see, a complex building, full of secret spaces and ingeniously concealed solutions to particular problems.

Most of all the story of building St Paul's is the story of human endeavour and a reminder that any construction project is not the work of one individual, but of a very large number of people working together over decades to produce the remarkable structure that still dominates the London skyline over three hundred years after it was completed.

1

A NEW DOME FOR LONDON

On 26 October 1708, a few days after Sir Christopher Wren's seventy-sixth birthday, a small group of men gathered on the scaffolding high above the London skyline to lay the last stone on the lantern of St Paul's Cathedral. It was a simple ceremony, with Christopher Wren junior, the son of the architect, deputizing for his father, accompanied by Edward Strong, the Master Mason, and Strong's son, also called Edward.

The elderly Surveyor was now too frail to climb the ladders; for the last few years he had been hoisted up in a basket to inspect progress on the dome. But this precarious method of ascent to the top of the lantern, over 300 feet (91 m) above the floor of the cathedral, was probably deemed too dangerous. It was all the more so since the outer timber dome had yet to be erected, so that the lantern, on which the last stone was being laid, appeared to perch precariously on a steep cone of brickwork towering over early eighteenth-century London.

This ceremony did not mark the end of construction: in 1708 there was still considerable work to be done, particularly on the west front. Indeed, it is difficult to pinpoint an exact date for the end of the works. Although the building would be declared officially complete on Christmas Day 1711, finishing touches were still being added ten years later. Nonetheless, the event that took place in 1708 was significant.

The small gathering on the lantern is not mentioned in any of the records in the cathedral archives. We only know that it took place at all from a short document written by the elder Edward Strong in May 1716. Perhaps it was a private event, attended only by those directly involved in the actual process of building; but its omission from official records may also be an indication of the growing tensions between the architect and the commissioners that were soon to break out into open hostility.[1]

By 1708 Sir Christopher Wren had been engaged on the cathedral in one capacity or another for over forty-five years. He was one of the few people alive who had seen the laying of the foundation stone thirty-three years before. Kings and queens had come and gone and the original master craftsmen, the deans and the bishops had all long since passed away. Those years of construction had, of course, not been without incident, and the architect may have paused to think back over the events that had led up to this day and remembered those friends and colleagues who had devoted so much of their lives to the building. What no one doubted at this point was that the construction of the cathedral was a remarkable achievement.

The cathedral they had built was formidably expensive. Accounts for 1716 show that the total amount of money passing through the cathedral books was a staggering £1,157,782 10s. 2½d. A million pounds was a huge amount of money in the early eighteenth century, all the more extraordinary when one realizes that the country had been on the verge of bankruptcy for decades on account of wars with France. As we shall see, raising such a vast sum had been a major problem throughout the works and shortfalls in income had been repeatedly responsible for delaying its completion.[2]

The new cathedral had originally been conceived as not only the largest building in London, but also one of the first domed buildings in England. Wren had seen domes on the Continent: there were several in Paris when he visited in 1665–66; there were also examples in Holland that he may have seen at first hand; and there were many in Italy that he presumably knew from his large collection of engravings. During his career Wren himself had been responsible for the construction of domes over several buildings including some of the City churches and Chelsea Hospital. He had designed many more that had got no further than the drawing board. The dome of St Paul's, however, was on a much grander scale than any other example in Great Britain, and would outshine other buildings for centuries to come. It also boasted a unique structure that had no precedent in architectural history and that has never been repeated. Its design was the result of Wren's scientific ingenuity, its peculiar position and the circumstances of its construction; and it was built using techniques that had probably not been used before in Northern Europe and were certainly new to England. But the dome is not the only place where Wren introduced structural innovations: the building is full of ingenious solutions to particular problems.

Wren is by far England's most famous architect. Indeed, he is one of the few architects who can be named by most members of the general public. Even during his lifetime he was famous, and his reputation, then as now, rested chiefly on his achievements at St Paul's. Strangely, despite his fame, his personal life is not particularly well documented. Much of what we know comes from a notoriously unreliable book entitled *Parentalia, or Memoirs of the Family of the Wrens*, compiled by his son Christopher and published by his grandson Stephen in 1750. Wren himself wrote no books and kept no journals.

To trace the lives of the craftsmen and office staff at the cathedral, we have to rely almost entirely on the records in the cathedral archives now preserved in the London Metropolitan Archives. The papers relating to the building of the cathedral consist of over a hundred volumes of contracts, letters, minutes and building accounts, detailing day-to-day life on site during its construction. As such, they form one of the most complete records of a seventeenth-century building site anywhere in the world.

They show us how much the workers were paid; they tell us how long they worked and how often; they provide details of the tools and methods the workers used and the problems they encountered; and they document the injuries and deaths, the scandals and corruption, the successes and the failures.

The story of the cathedral's construction that these documents reveal – and indeed the whole idea of building a new dome over London – starts with the old St Paul's and the restoration of the monarchy in 1660.

The old cathedral was not the first, nor even the second, but at least the fourth to be built on that spot. Indeed, there has probably been a St Paul's Cathedral on the same site for over 1,400 years. The first, constructed in AD 604, burned down in 675. The second was destroyed by

A view of Old St Paul's after Inigo Jones's extensive alterations to the external façades, showing his celebrated portico at the west entrance, and St Gregory's Church, which stood beside the west end; from William Dugdale's *History of St Paul's Cathedral* (1658).

the Vikings in 962, and the third by another fire in 1087. The medieval cathedral, begun by the Normans and finished in 1327, had been a magnificent building, but it had long since fallen into disrepair. In the early seventeenth century, as a celebration of Charles I's rule, Inigo Jones had attempted some aesthetic improvements, recladding the nave and transepts and constructing a magnificent new portico at its west end. Oliver Cromwell had torn down the statues on the portico in 1650 and used the building as a barracks and as stabling for horses. By 1660 it was in a very sorry state.[3]

The newly restored King Charles II saw in the rebuilding of St Paul's an important opportunity to re-establish his authority and the dignity of the Crown. It was with this aim that in 1661, a year after his restoration, he sought advice over the building's stability. The person to whom he turned was a highly gifted young professor of astronomy at Oxford called Christopher Wren.[4]

2

THE ASTRONOMER ARCHITECT

We are not sure exactly how Christopher Wren's first became involved with St Paul's. At the time, he was a well-known mathematician and academic. He held the distinguished position of Savilian Professor of Astronomy at the University of Oxford and was one of the founding members of the Royal Society. Despite all these achievements, today we would consider him an odd person to approach with an architectural problem. Yet the king's choice reveals much about the architect's role three and a half centuries ago and about preferment in the Restoration court. To understand it, we must consider both the type of people who practised architecture in the seventeenth century and Wren's own background.

The first difference between a modern architect and his seventeenth-century counterpart is one of training. Today, an architect is a university-educated professional who is expected to have an in-depth knowledge of building construction and design. In the seventeenth century, however, there was no such thing as a formal architectural education. Although academies existed in France, the first architecture school on this side of the English Channel – the Architectural Association – was not set up until 1847. Before that date, if an Englishman received any sort of training as an architect it was through being apprenticed to someone already in the profession.[1]

The second difference between modern and seventeenth-century practice lies in the architect's role. When working on simple buildings, architects today might handle every part of the design themselves, but on more complicated projects they usually rely on other specialists to help them with the various technical aspects of the design. Structural engineers calculate the loading of the beams and design the structural elements; services engineers determine the layout of pipes, ducts and cables; quantity surveyors keep an eye on the costs; and project managers try to keep the whole scheme on budget and on schedule. In the seventeenth century none of these supporting specializations existed: structural engineers, quantity surveyors, project managers and services engineers did not appear as separate professions until the twentieth century.

Another difference was one of status. In the seventeenth century the place of the architect in society was chiefly founded on contemporary practice in Italy and France, which in turn was based on the architect's role as set out in the earliest surviving treatise on the subject: Vitruvius's *Ten Books on Architecture*, written sometime late in the first century BC. Vitruvius described architects as a masters of arts and sciences, distinguishing them from artisans. This made architecture a respectable profession for scholarly study and a fit occupation for gentlemen, but this notion – taken up enthusiastically by Renaissance scholars on the Continent – was slow to catch on in England. It is not until Inigo Jones (1573–1652), who had travelled widely in Italy, that we find anyone we might be able to consider an architect in this sense, and throughout the sixteenth century the English architectural scene had remained essentially medieval in its conception, with master craftsmen being responsible for both the design and the construction of buildings. After Jones, an increasing number of people began to practise as architects. Some were craftsmen who specialized in making drawings and who sought respectability, such as Edward Marshall (*c.* 1598–1675) and William Townesend (1676–1739). Others were gentlemen who started by building for themselves and then – as their results were admired – offered their services to others: figures such as Roger North (1653–1734) and Sir Roger Pratt (1620–85). There was also a small number of men who had received some kind of training with other architects and who went into architecture as a career from the beginning: John Webb (1611–72) and Nicholas Hawksmoor (1662?–1736) fit into this last category. Most buildings had no architect as such. The profession had no clear identity in this period, and no distinction was made between the amateur and the professional.[2]

The final difference between modern and seventeenth-century conceptions of the field was one of definition. English library catalogues of the period categorized architecture as a branch of mathematics. This idea is less surprising when one considers the fact that most architectural books were concerned either with illustrating proportional systems for determining the ratios of the different parts to the orders of Classical architecture, or with explaining methods of surveying. Land surveying had risen to prominence after the dissolution of the monasteries under Henry VIII, and surveyors made a good living settling disputes between rival landowners by drawing maps and plans. Throughout seventeenth-century England the terms 'surveyor' and 'architect' remained pretty much synonymous. On his own projects Wren was always appointed and referred to as 'the Surveyor of the Works' and not 'the Architect'. And as we shall see, a thorough mastery of mathematics – albeit combined with artistic ability – was a prerequisite for anyone who designed buildings.

When Wren's assistance was sought in 1661 he would not have called himself an architect, and certainly no one at the time would have guessed that the young professor of astronomy would be remembered for architecture rather than for his scientific achievements. He had built absolutely nothing, but he was already well known as one of the most successful of a new breed of experimental philosophers. Wren was at the cutting edge of this new field, and the king must have sought his advice because they were acquainted (the king had already promoted Wren to the Savilian Professorship), because Wren was well known for solving practical problems, and – since the problem in hand was seen as essentially mathematical in nature – because Wren had a reputation as a brilliant mathematician.

Wren had been born into a loyal High Church family in the quiet village of East Knoyle in Wiltshire in October 1632. He was named after his father, the village's rector, whose brother Matthew Wren would be elevated from dean of Windsor to bishop of Hereford, and then Ely, only a few years later. It was Bishop Matthew who persuaded the Crown to appoint his brother as the new dean of Windsor in his place. The new job came with a residence, and thus the young Christopher Wren spent most of his childhood not in an isolated village in Wiltshire but in Windsor Castle. It is completely possible that as a young boy he met the young princes who were later to become Charles II and James II: they were of a similar age.[3]

The young Wren was a rather sickly child and had to be educated mostly at home, although he seems to have been sent briefly to Westminster School, possibly to put him in a place of relative safety in a time of great uncertainty.[4] The Civil War was a disaster for the family. Wren's father had lost his post and his house was sacked twice. He was forced to seek refuge first in Knoyle and then in Bletchingdon near Oxford, where his son-in-law William Holder was rector. Bishop Matthew Wren fared even worse: he was imprisoned in the Tower of London for the entire Interregnum. His father's forced exile had one advantage for young Christopher: it brought him under the influence of his brother-in-law William Holder, an intellectual and mathematician who tutored Christopher in geometry.[5] In 1647 the young man's ill health also brought him into the care of Charles Scarbrugh, who took him on as a laboratory assistant. Wren proved a highly able pupil, and at the age of fifteen or sixteen translated into Latin a tract on the design of sundials for the mathematician William Oughtred. It was probably through his interest in sundials that he first became involved in astronomy. Through Holder and Scarbrugh Wren met other scientists, and by the time he went up to Oxford he already had a good grounding in geometry, anatomy, Latin and Greek, and already knew many of the leading scientists of the age. There is even a suggestion that he might have gone abroad at this time in the company of John Wallis, a mathematician, cryptographer and courtier who was travelling in the entourage of the young Elector Palatine, returning to Heidelberg at the end of the Thirty Years War, although this is not widely accepted.[6]

Wren's exceptional abilities were apparent at university: he went up to Wadham College, Oxford, in 1649, took his Bachelor of Arts degree in 1651, received his Master of Arts in 1653, and the same year was elected a Fellow of All Souls College. There he remained until 1657, when he was chosen as the Professor of Astronomy of Gresham College in London at the remarkably young age of twenty-five.[7]

At Oxford, Wren – no doubt benefiting from introductions from Holder and from his father's connections – had been fortunate enough to fall into the company of a group of men who were at the forefront of scientific research. They included Seth Ward (later to become bishop of Salisbury), Robert Boyle (famous for Boyle's Law), Ralph Bathurst (later Master of Trinity College, Oxford), William Petty (who had made a fortune organizing a survey of Ireland), Thomas Willis (who would later become Sedleian Professor of Natural Philosophy at Oxford) and Robert Hooke. Wren was highly regarded by his contemporaries both for his intelligence and for his manual dexterity. He could draw beautifully and was able to construct intricate instruments and models for experiments and demonstrations. His abilities extended to the art of dissection, allowing him to take part in some of the ground-breaking anatomical studies into the circulation of the blood being carried out at the time.[8]

In reading through accounts of this period, one cannot help but be struck by the extraordinary range of Wren's interests and the scientific advances he made. He carried out some of the first intravenous injections, produced a theory for the rings of Saturn and wrote a mathematical proof for the rectification of the cycloid (the arc traced by a point on the circumference of a wheel rolling along a line); he invented devices for surveying, musical and acoustical instruments, new ways of fishing, methods of constructing underwater and of submarine navigation; and he also carried out experiments in printmaking. In 1661 he was given two assignments by the Crown in the field of optics: the first, which he carried out himself, was to construct a giant globe of the moon; the second was to create a book of engravings of observations through a microscope – a project that Wren started but then entrusted to his great friend Robert Hooke, who published the results as *Micrographia* in 1665. Perhaps most significantly, it was Wren and Hooke who first came up with the idea that gravity obeyed an inverse square law, and who persuaded Edmund Halley to approach Newton to find the proof.[9]

The Gresham Professorship, which Wren had received in 1657, had come through his Oxford connections, and it gave the young man a place to live in London. Gresham College had been founded by Sir Thomas Gresham in 1597 to provide continuing education for businessmen in the City of London. It had professors in geometry, theology, astronomy, medicine and law. Each was expected to lecture once a week in Latin and once a week in English in return for rooms in the college and a stipend. The group of scientists to which Wren had belonged in Oxford was part of a larger circle that had met in London before the Civil War. Now, in the late 1650s, Gresham College provided a focus for the club, which would later decide to call itself the Royal Society.[10]

The Commonwealth crumbled after Oliver Cromwell's death in 1658, his son Richard proving an ineffectual leader. The restoration of the monarchy in 1660 saw a complete reshuffling of public offices. Those who had been given any sort of major post in the Protectorate were now obliged to relinquish it. In such a climate there were opportunities for advancement for ambitious younger men if they could get themselves noticed. In August, only days after the king had made Bruno Ryves his new Register of the Garter, Wren seized the opportunity to have an audience with the king in order to return the precious Garter Record Book his father had hidden. At the same time his acquaintances were working behind the scenes to secure the young Wren a more important post.[11]

An opportunity soon presented itself. Seth Ward, one of Wren's scientific mentors, was removed from the prestigious Savilian Professorship in Astronomy at Oxford to be given a clerical post from which he would later rise to become bishop of Salisbury. Wren's supporters (Ward included) managed to have him named as Ward's successor. Wren duly resigned his professorship at Gresham College in March and was installed in his new chair on 15 May 1661. Meanwhile his uncle Matthew was restored as bishop of Ely, and his cousin (also called Matthew) became secretary first to Edward Hyde, Earl of Clarendon, and subsequently to the Duke of York (later James II). Letters show that by 1661 Christopher Wren was beginning to move regularly in Court circles. In August he found a further excuse to meet the king, this time presenting the lunar globe on which he had been working.[12] Indeed, Wren may have been spending too much time in London: the first reference we have to his involvement with St Paul's Cathedral occurs in a letter from a friend in Wadham College, Thomas Sprat, warning Wren in 1661 that the vice chancellor was concerned that Wren was neglecting his duties as Savilian Professor.[13]

Wren's involvement with St Paul's may have been suggested to the king by Gilbert Sheldon, newly installed as bishop of London. Like Wren and his father before him, Sheldon was a staunch royalist. He had served Charles I and had been with him during his retreat to the Isle of Wight; he had also been ejected by Parliament from his post as Warden of All Souls College in 1648. Another connection that may have aided Wren's advancement was his cousin Matthew, the son of Bishop Matthew

Wren. Wren had provided him and his brother Thomas with a place to live in Oxford while their father was imprisoned in the Tower of London, and Matthew knew John Barwick, who would be made dean of St Paul's in 1661.[14]

In the years that followed Wren became increasingly interested in the design of buildings and began to received his first architectural commissions. The first was a new chapel commissioned by his uncle Matthew Wren for Pembroke College, Cambridge, and completed between 1663 and 1665. The second, which arrived through his Oxford connections, was for a new building to house degree ceremonies. The idea for such a place had originally been put forward by Archbishop Laud and shelved during the Interregnum, but it was now being resurrected thanks to a large donation from Sheldon. The Sheldonian Theatre, as it became known, was designed and constructed between 1663 and 1669.[15]

In 1661–63, while Wren was busy designing buildings in Oxford and Cambridge, lecturing and carrying out experiments, little progress was being made on repair work on Old St Paul's. The problem was probably one of finance. At that time the cathedral repairs were under the control of the Office of the King's Works, but Charles II lived lavishly. He spent wildly on entertaining and on mistresses, and he generally lived hopelessly beyond his allowance. It seems there was no money left over for a new cathedral. After two years, the best solution for St Paul's that could be found was the creation of a Royal Commission in 1663. This at least made the cathedral independent: the commissioners were empowered to take advice where they wished, demolish as they saw fit and – most importantly – to raise money. In practice, they delegated most of their powers to a much smaller group of interested parties centred around the dean, the bishop of London and the archbishop of Canterbury.[16]

The commissioners' first act was once more to assess the cathedral's physical condition. In July 1664 they sought the advice of experts in the King's Works: Sir John Denham (Surveyor of the King's Works and a poet), Edward Marshall (Master Mason of the King's Works) and John Webb (architect and pupil of Inigo Jones). The conclusion they collectively reached was that the tower was unstable and needed to be demolished without delay. Before any money had been raised, the rather impetuous Webb had already begun to procure timber for scaffolding.[17]

The commissioners, perhaps wary of the cost and the scale of the task that faced them, sought a second opinion in January 1665. Their new expert was Roger Pratt, a gentleman turned architect who had been responsible for a number of country houses during the Interregnum and who was currently constructing a handsome mansion for the Earl of Clarendon. Pratt turned out to be rather conservative. In his report he recommended keeping the whole church and patching it up. That may have suited the commissioners, who wanted a realistic project, but it can hardly have satisfied either Charles II or Sheldon, who had just been promoted to the office of archbishop of Canterbury, both of whom were looking for a symbol of the newly restored monarchy. Nor can it have pleased the new dean, William Sancroft. As a result, nothing was done until the following year.[18]

While the commissioners delayed and the dean settled into his new appointment, Wren was in France, where he spent nine months in 1665–66. Lectures at the University of Oxford had been suspended because of the plague, so he had taken the opportunity to visit French scientists and to see the country's remarkable architecture. He even managed a brief interview with the Italian sculptor and architect Gianlorenzo Bernini, and he brought back bundles of engravings of French and Italian architecture.[19]

When Wren returned to England, the commission asked him to prepare yet another report on the state of the cathedral. No doubt inspired by the exciting new architecture he had seen being constructed all over Paris, in his report of 1 May 1666 Wren was damning of suggestions for saving the tower. He favoured its demolition. However, he also

Wren's pre-Fire design for adding a dome to the old cathedral. It was designed to be constructed around the existing tower, which would then be demolished. The arches of the Romanesque nave can be seen on the left and those of the Gothic choir on the right.

realized that Londoners would be concerned if they saw their precious cathedral being altered, so he came up with an ingenious proposal for building a new tower around the old. When the new structure had reached sufficient height – and looked sufficiently impressive to placate the public – the old one inside could be demolished from within, unseen and unremarked by anyone outside. In August of that year he produced drawings of just such a design, showing St Paul's with a dome surmounted by a dramatic spire in the shape of a pine cone (see Plate 4) or pineapple. The suggestion, often made by historians, that it is a pineapple as an emblem of welcome is doubtful. It is more likely to have been intended as a reference to the bronze pine cone of unknown origin that had stood outside at the doors of St Peter's and that was a symbol of Rome.[20]

On Monday 27 August the commissioners met once more at St Paul's to discuss the way forward. Those present now included the bishop of London (Humphrey Henchman), the dean (William Sancroft), Wren, Roger Pratt, Hugh May, John Evelyn, Thomas Chichley (Commissioner and Master of the Ordnance), Henry Slingsby (Master of the Mint) and several 'expert workmen'. Chichley and Pratt proposed repair, while Evelyn and Wren both supported the idea of demolishing the tower and building a dome in its place (Wren no doubt having in mind the drawings he had already prepared). Evelyn notes in his diary that after much discussion his and Wren's view was accepted.[21]

The message Wren's design sent out was clear: the new dome, the first to be constructed in England, would form the architectural centrepiece of a London rebuilt to rival and surpass ancient Rome. His plan would undoubtedly have pleased the king, but it did not matter. In less than a week, both the great City that was to be the new Rome and the old cathedral that was to be at its centrepiece were completely destroyed.

3

FIRE AND DESTRUCTION

The commissioners' meeting at St Paul's, which Wren had attended, took place on Monday 27 August 1666. The following Saturday, 1 September, a baker in Pudding Lane, about half a mile to the east of St Paul's, tamped out the embers in his ovens as he did every evening and went to bed. By three in the morning he was scrambling for his life across the roofs, away from his burning shop.[1]

From the baker's shop, the fire spread at a terrifying rate through the closely packed timber-framed houses of the City. All attempts to put it out were to no avail, and by the afternoon of the third day (Tuesday) the cathedral itself was threatened. St Paul's Churchyard had long been a centre for the bookselling trade; the bishop kindly gave the merchants, who were members of the Stationers' Company, permission to secure their precious wares in the crypt. St Faith's, which occupied the under-croft, was the Stationers' Company church. Here, beneath the choir – apparently protected by the fire-proof stone vaults above – thousands of books were swiftly stacked by panicking booksellers before they packed up the rest of their possessions and fled. On Tuesday evening, as the flames approached, the houses alongside the cathedral caught alight, and then the scaffolding around the tower, which in turn carried the flames to the roof. The books in the crypt caught fire and the church was doomed.[2]

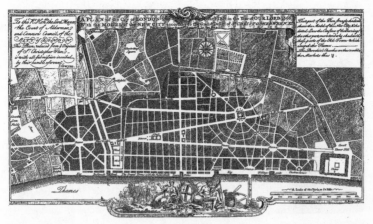

Wren's plan for rebuilding the City of London after the Great Fire, drawn in September 1666.

The Great Fire of London burned for four days. It is estimated that during that time it managed to destroy 13,200 houses, 87 parish churches, 6 consecrated chapels, 52 livery halls, the Guildhall, the Royal Exchange, the Customs House, Newgate Prison and three City gates. Remarkably, only six people died, but the conflagration had rendered 80,000–100,000 inhabitants homeless and destroyed an area of some 373 acres (150 hectares). It had reduced virtually everything within the old City walls to smouldering ruins.[3]

Just six days after the fire, Wren sought an audience with the king. He was bearing his design for rebuilding the City. Where the old City had been maze of twisted alleyways and narrow streets, Wren's plan showed a regular arrangement of broad boulevards linking key buildings with a logical pattern of smaller streets between. It was a bold vision, but it would never come to pass. The authorities quickly concluded that the redistribution of lots it would entail was too complicated. Nevertheless, it clearly signalled Wren's interest in rebuilding to the authorities.[4]

As the buildings still smouldered, the cathedral authorities took stock of the situation. Bishop Henchman and Dean Sancroft called in Wren and asked him to survey what was left of the great cathedral and to give his verdict on what should now be done. Although John Evelyn, Roger Pratt and John Denham had all been consulted before the fire, now it was to Wren alone that the commissioners turned.[5]

Wren delivered his report on the cathedral in January or February of 1667, some four or five months after the fire. In it, he describes how the the roofs covering the aisles, the nave, both transepts and the choir had all been destroyed. The vault of the choir crypt, which housed St Faith's Church, had also collapsed, and very little of the walls remained. He reported that in the body of the church more of the walls and arches were standing, but the remains of the tower were in a very dangerous condition, with stones raining down on passers-by. He noted that the stone of the great portico designed by Inigo Jones was so splintered that the whole structure was structurally unsafe and utterly beyond repair.[6]

The dean and bishop had also asked Wren to report on the possibility of erecting a temporary building in what remained of the choir so that services could resume as soon as possible. Wren was dismissive of this suggestion, noting that there was so little of the choir remaining it would be expensive and would require the digging out of the crypt. He also pointed out that such a building would sit under the shadow of the tower, which in his view was in danger of collapsing. He suggested erecting a temporary roof over part of the nave instead, where the existing north and south doors could be used for access. By this strategy, he went on, it might be possible to construct something that might stand firm for centuries. Nonetheless, he remained generally unenthusiastic about repairing the old cathedral, saying that trying to do so would 'be like the mending of the Argo Navis, scarce anything will at last be left of the old'.[7]

Despite Wren's advice, a year later in January 1668, the commissioners issued an order for the erection of a temporary choir within the nave and for the walling-in of the site. The contract for the new roof was signed with Thomas Gammon, carpenter, in March. They managed to erect timber walling to keep the public out of the ruins, but work then stopped as Wren's prediction about the building's dangerous condition was proved to be accurate.[8]

After the commissioners had started work on the nave, readying it to receive the new roof, it had become clear that the cathedral was less stable than they had hoped, and the whole fabric had started to break apart. In April 1668 Dean Sancroft wrote to Wren in Oxford reporting that the work about the west end 'is fallen about our ears' and summoning him urgently to London to advise on what was to be done about the remainder of the cathedral. Henceforth all thoughts of patching up the old structure were abandoned and all efforts turned to the design of a replacement.[9]

4

MODELS, DESIGNS
AND WARRANTS

On 2 July 1668, a few months after Wren's help had been sought with the problem of falling masonry, Dean Sancroft again summoned him from Oxford, this time asking him 'to prepare something to be proposed to his Majesty (the Design of a Quire, at least, as may be a congruous Part of a greater and more magnificent Work to follow)'. John Denham, the Surveyor of the King's Works and official Surveyor of St Paul's, was ordered by the king to make Wren his deputy in March 1669. Denham died only a few weeks later, and on 29 March Wren was appointed Surveyor of the King's Works in his place. On 30 July 1669 Wren was finally officially appointed Surveyor to the Fabric of St Paul's, a role he had effectively been carrying out for several years.[1]

In his plan of 1666 for the rebuilding of London after the Great Fire, Wren had already shown a small domed structure in place of St Paul's. It is not clear exactly how his ideas developed between 1668 and 1669, but the problems surrounding the cost of any future building seem to have been uppermost in his mind. During all the discussions of shoring up the old walls, there seemed to be a general concern that the Church would not be able to afford a new cathedral for a long time, and that when it did so the new structure would have to be considerably smaller than the original.

One of the earliest schemes we have from this period is in the form of a model and it is thus always referred to as the 'First Model design'. A single sectional drawing has also now been identified as relating to it. Wren worked out the First Model design in the autumn of 1669. The model itself was made out of oak and pear wood by the joiner William Cleere, with carving by his brother Robert. It took at least three months to put together and was completed in March 1670 at a cost of £250 15s. Wren was paid 100 guineas 'in gold' for his work on the design; and the accounts also list charges of £2 in March/April 1670 for the transport of the model to Whitehall, where it was shown to King Charles, and £1 10s. for its return two years later in June 1672. Half of this model survives and is on display in the cathedral to this day. The other half is sadly missing. It was probably the more interesting part and the difference in transport costs may indicate that it was kept in Whitehall by the king.[2]

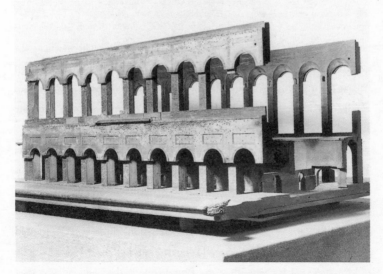

The remains of the First Model, still on display in the Trophy Room at St Paul's. It shows the proposed choir of the new cathedral; the domed entrance vestibule is missing.

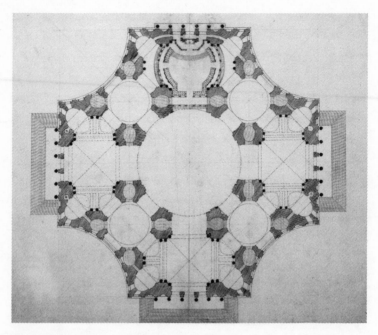

The plan of the Greek cross design showing the choir placed on the east side of the dome. The Baroque concave elevations would have been unique in England.

The model's surviving section shows the proposed choir, where the services would have been held. It is a very curious design. The architect Roger Pratt saw the whole model on 12 July 1673 and observed that it was different from any previous cathedral in its lack of transepts or nave. He was particularly scathing of the arcades that Wren had positioned on the outside of the choir on either side. Wren presumably designed these for the booksellers who had traditionally sold their wares around the cathedral, but Pratt called them 'useless porticos', also objecting to the position of the dome at the west end and its separation from the nave. The commissioners seem to have agreed with him: they concluded that the design was 'not stately enough' and asked Wren to return to the drawing board.[3]

Parentalia tells us that while the First Model languished in Whitehall between 1670 and 1672, Wren produced a number of drawings for

A section of the Greek cross design showing a double dome with sloping walls, which is strikingly similar to the cathedral as executed.

'discourse sake'. By far the most interesting to survive is a scheme for a dramatic centralized church. This was probably inspired by early designs for St Peter's in Rome. In plan, it was symmetrical with three of the four sides containing entrances and that last side housing the altar and a circular choir. The centre was covered by a huge dome. The 'Greek cross design', as it is called, was approved by the king in November 1672, and an order was issued in December 1672 for the construction of a model to be built so big that 'a Man might stand within it'. Before the model was started, in February 1673, Hooke reported that Wren had added a library vestibule and a portico to the west end. It was to this modified plan, now known as the 'Great Model design', that the model was actually constructed.[4]

The Great Model (Plate 3) that Wren built for the king is still on display in the cathedral today and is one of the finest architectural models ever made. Between April and September 1673 Wren, aided by Edward Woodroffe, started scaling up the drawings, and work on the model itself commenced. By February 1674 Robert Hooke was able to walk inside it, but it was not completed until the following September. It was scaled to 1 inch to 2 feet (1:24) and was 13 feet (3.95 m) high, 13 feet 1 inch (3.97 m) wide and 20 feet 11 inches (6.36 m) long. The model was raised on a platform so that its ground level was at waist height. Internally, most of the floor was missing so that visitors could 'walk around' inside it. Although it was made out of wood, both the interior and the exterior were originally plastered and painted, and the whole was finished with £5 worth of gilding, trompe-l'oeil painted vaults and eighteen miniature statues. The total expenditure was over £500, as much as it cost to build a small house in London and equivalent to several hundred thousand pounds in today's terms.[5]

Wren was particularly proud of the Great Model: *Parentalia* records that 'upon Recollection ... the Surveyor in private conversation, always seem'd to set a higher Value on this Design, than any he had made before or since'. Once it had been put on display, however, criticism seems to have flooded in. His son recalled that the 'Chapter, and some others of the Clergy thought that the Model [was] not enough of a Cathedral-fashion; to instance particularly, in that the Quire was design'd Circular'. Of greater concern, however, was the fact that the choir had been placed within the structure of the dome, meaning that it could not have been built separately. The principle that the works could be phased, with the choir being completed before the rest of the building, was seen as critical. Since it was unclear at this stage how the cathedral would be financed, a building that could be completed in stages had obvious advantages.[6]

In 1674 Wren started to work on new designs, this time concentrating on more traditional groundplans. A number of unsuccessful schemes survive, but finally he hit on one that appeared to meet all the conflicting

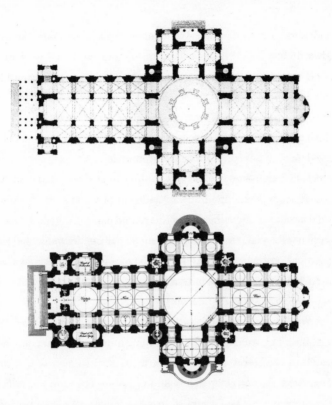

The Warrant design (top) compared with a plan of the cathedral as built.

criteria. This design, submitted to Whitehall sometime in early 1675, was approved by royal warrant and is thus called the 'Warrant' design. It is frequently said that the royal warrant included a clause allowing Wren to make any changes he wished. This originates from a misreading of *Parentalia*, and no such clause existed in the warrant itself. It is, however, possible that Wren might have been given separate permission to make changes. The original warrant of the commission (rather than the one that accompanied the Warrant design) allowed the commissioners to build a new cathedral as they wished, so it is equally possible that Wren, as their appointed architect, might have taken this to mean that he too had the right to alter the design. What is certain is that changes were indeed made.[7]

The Warrant design differs in a number of key ways from the cathedral as built:

- The layout of the pillars and towers around the dome crossing is different.
- No crypt is shown.
- The walls are thinner.
- The transepts end in rectangular porches.
- The section shows no screen walls above the aisles, meaning that the buttresses supporting the roof would have been visible from outside the cathedral.
- The west end is much simpler, without the extensions that hold the Consistory Court, Library, Morning Chapel and Trophy Room.
- The towers are different, and the portico is similar to the one Inigo Jones built for Charles II.
- The Warrant design features an extraordinary dome.

While the Warrant design was awaiting approval in Whitehall, Wren continued to adjust the plans. This period of the new cathedral's genesis has excited considerable debate among architectural historians. Some have suggested that by the end of 1675 Wren must have already decided on the design more or less as it was built, with only a few areas, such as the dome and the western towers, left to be finalized. But more recent scholarship suggests that when he began construction, he was probably still working to something much closer to the original Warrant design, and that his ideas at this stage for the upper parts of the cathedral were radically different from what was finally executed.[8]

Wren's willingness to start a building whose design was not fixed should not surprise us much. At this early stage his priority was to determine the position of the great piers in the choir and the legs of the dome. As the crypt had to be built first, it would be several years before detailed designs were needed for the walls above ground in the east end, allowing plenty of time for adjustments to be made. The west end would

A longitudinal section through the Warrant design, showing its strange multitiered dome.

not be constructed for decades. Such a way of working would be unthink-
able today because the costs of building construction – and thus the form
of the building itself – are fixed by contract before any work begins on
site. As we shall see, Wren had no such limitations. He specifically organ-
ized the works so that his design could be continually refined and
adjusted. Nothing needed to be fixed until it was built. What mattered
at the beginning was to make sure no decisions were taken now that
would create problems later on. Some elements of the design did have
to be fixed – the spacing of the piers, the diameter of the dome, the size
of its supporting piers and the overall dimensions of the east end –
because they in turn affected the size of columns on the outside of the
building, but the detailed design of such elements could wait until

later. Many of the plan's key features are easier to understand in this light. With this in mind, we might easily suppose that the earlier designs were somehow irrelevant. In fact, the opposite was true. As we shall see, Wren's ability to change the design enabled him to return to ideas that had initially been rejected by the commissioners. The final cathedral would owe much more to these early schemes than anyone at the time would have guessed.

The royal warrant allowing work to begin was formally issued on 14 May 1675. The foundation stone was laid thirty-eight days later, on 21 June 1675. In the meantime the site had not been idle: while Wren was working on his designs, demolition had been under way for some years.[9]

5

THE DEMOLITION MEN

When Wren had visited the site in May 1668, after receiving Dean Sancroft's letter of 25 April concerning the collapse of the upper parts of the west end, he reported to the dean that he thought that it was a 'miracle' that the tower was still standing. On 2 July he had again been summoned from Oxford, this time to meet the commissioners to discuss what was to be done. A royal warrant was issued three weeks later, on 25 July 1668, allowing demolition to begin. In August 1668 the commissioners ordered the remainder of the choir and the crossing tower to be dismantled.[1]

Some demolition and stabilization of the fabric had been carried out immediately after the Great Fire. In September 1667 masons had been paid to suspend themselves from ropes and knock down any masonry that appeared to be in danger of falling from the high vaults of the nave and choir. A wall 10 feet (3 m) high had been built around the west end of the cathedral and its south side to secure this part of the site and to ensure that any good stone or other reusable building materials could be stacked up there. But the main focus of the work in 1667 and early 1668 was the strengthening of the existing pillars and the removal of debris to allow the intended temporary choir to be constructed in the nave.[2]

Labourers formed the backbone of operations at St Paul's, particularly in these early years. In October 1668 forty-five labourers worked a

total of 969 days, an average of 21 days each for that month. The basic
working week in the seventeenth century was six days long, with only
Sunday reserved as a day of rest. However, numerous religious festivals
were celebrated as public holidays, so the average month amounted to
only 22–23 working days. The days themselves were long and arduous.
All building workers were expected to arrive on site at 6 am. Workers
were not meant to leave the site for lunch, which was around midday, and
the Clerk of the Cheque used an hour-glass to make sure that they did
not take too long over their meal. Work began again at 1 pm and continued until 6 pm. Working hours were marked by a bell that had been
taken down from the old cathedral and re-erected for the purpose in
Convocation House Yard next to the office of works. All workers going
on and off site at St Paul's were noted in a register at the Call Booth,
which was next to the office of works on the south side of the cathedral.
A mark was made in the register in the morning and a second one in the
afternoon, so that each labourer was paid for either a whole or a half day.
The labourers also had to check out at the end of each day.[3]

The labourers were the lowest-paid workers on site. In 1668 their
wages were 1s. 4d. a day, with their foreman John Chrismas being paid 2s.
a day. As we shall see in later chapters, it is possible that most took home
even less, but calculations of the cost of living at the time show that these
labourers would have struggled to survive even if they had taken home
the full 1s. 4d.[4]

The accounts for St Paul's painstakingly list the names of every
labourer present on site each day, together with the number of days he
worked each month. The use of the word 'he' here is deliberate, because
few female names appear in the lists of labourers or tradesmen for the
years 1665–1718. For the most part the only women mentioned are
widows who were being paid sums owed to them for work done by their
husbands before they had died. Elsewhere in this period widows occasionally took over their husbands' businesses and ran them very

successfully, but this never seems to have happened at St Paul's. The only example of a female tradesman being employed for her own skills was Jane Brewer, the foundress who cast the brass pineapple on top of the south-west tower and carried out various other works from 1707–8.[5]

Labourers were employed in menial tasks throughout the cathedral's construction – predominantly digging, lifting and carrying. To help them work effectively, the office supplied wheelbarrows, pulleys, axes, crowbars, picks and spades. The number of labourers working at any one time varied greatly. In winter months the days were short – it got light only at 8 am and was dark by 4 pm – and it was also too cold to do much on site. Indeed, the winters of 1678–79, 1680–81 and 1683–84 were so cold that

The west end of the cathedral during demolition, showing the high wall built to screen off the site and allow for the storage of materials. Drawing by Thomas Wyck, *c.* 1672.

the Thames froze over. During these months there were sometimes only a few labourers on site, but at the height of the main building season (which ran from April to September) there were typically 20 to 30. However, demolition was less dependent on the weather than most construction, and the highest number of labourers recorded for any month was 67, in February 1669.[6]

Between 1668 and 1675 the labourers' main tasks were to shift rubble and dig out the foundations. Good stone was sorted from the broken fragments. Most of the rubble consisted of Kentish ragstone – hard stone, quarried near Maidstone in Kent, that had been used as infill in the great medieval walls. Much of it was now bought by the City to be used for paving the streets, while the rest was stored to use in the rebuilding. Dirt, ashes and dust had to be removed completely, which was a huge task: in just two months of 1669, for example, no fewer that 1,250 carts of rubbish were transported down Ludgate Hill.[7]

One might have assumed that the task of demolishing the tower and higher walls would have fallen to the cathedral's labourers, but in fact it was let to subcontractors. Henry Russell signed a contract in August 1668 to pull down the upper parts of the tower at the rate of 40s. a yard (in October and November 1668 he was paid the sum of £50 for his pains), while Messrs T. Newton and J. Simpson undertook the demolition of the choir. *Parentalia* describes the methods that were used: 'The pulling down [of] the Walls, being about 80 Feet high, and 5 feet thick, was a great and troublesome Work; the Men stood above, and work'd them down with Pickaxes, whilst Labourers below moved away the Materials that fell, and dispersed them into Heaps.'[8]

The separation of the stones was probably not difficult since they were only held together with soft and friable lime mortar. Each layer could be pushed or lifted off the previous one, but the stones were heavy and often arranged in such a way that the removal of one could lead to the collapse of many others, endangering the workmen. These men were also working at considerable heights. Between 1668 and October 1673 three people were killed and three seriously injured, but the demolition was the most dangerous part of the work. The cathedral paid surgeons' fees, compensation to injured men and to widows, and the funeral expenses of those who died. Given the scale of the operations and lack of safety procedures, there were remarkably few fatalities. In the main forty-year period of construction, from 1675 to 1715, there were just six deaths, a record that would put most modern building sites to shame. To their credit, the cathedral authorities did what they could to help the families of those who had died or who were no longer able to work.[9]

By July 1671 the tower had been demolished down to the level of the great arches over the nave, and by the end of the year scaffolding had been erected to allow the rose window to be dismantled at the east end. However, the huge piers that had supported the tower presented a particular problem. Wren constructed a massive battering ram to demolish them, using a mast 40 feet (12 m) long tipped by an enormous iron spike. It was suspended by ropes attached to each end of the mast, and hung from a huge hoop supported by an A-frame of timber. It took thirty people to operate the ram, fifteen on each side pulling on ropes. Wren's son tells of how the workmen swung the ram back and forth for a whole day against the immovable bulk of one pier, seemingly with no effect; they despaired, but Wren encouraged them to continue, and on the second day the masonry trembled at the top and a few hours later collapsed. He claimed that the vibrations gradually loosened the stones, fracturing bonds until the structure failed. The ram worked but it was slow, so Wren decided to look for other methods.

After due deliberation Wren elected to use explosives. As far as we know, gunpowder was not commonly used for civilian demolitions. He was therefore understandably cautious, first seeking advice from a gunner at the Tower of London and then taking personal responsibility for the work.[10] Following Wren's instructions, labourers dug a hole beside the

A view across the east end of the cathedral after the demolition of the choir and tower. The remains of the nave can be seen on the right. (Note the interested mother and child exploring the site in the foreground.) Drawing by Thomas Wyck, *c.* 1672.

north-west pillar down to the foundations. They then tunnelled into the centre of the pillar, where they placed a deal box containing 18 lbs (8 kg) of gunpowder. This was attached by means of a wick and a train of gunpowder first passing through a cane and then running along the ground. The hole was then bricked up by the bricklayer Thomas Warren, and it was Warren who was paid to light the train and run.[11]

Wren's son later described how all those watching heard a loud explosion and saw the whole pillar lift nine inches into the air, breaking the great arches and the smaller ones to the side. It seemed to hang there for a moment and then came crashing down in a heap of rubble, shaking the ground like an earthquake. It was said at the time that the 18 lbs of powder had lifted 3,000 tons of masonry and saved the work of a thousand men. The experiment was a huge success. The method was repeated on the other piers of the tower and might have been used for the rest of the cathedral had it not been for an accident.[12]

The Surveyor had been called out of London 'on the King's Service'. *Parentalia* recalls how he left the work in charge of 'his next officer' (presumably his Assistant Surveyor, Edward Woodroffe), 'who too wise in his own conceit' put in much more powder and neither dug the tunnel deep enough nor bricked it up securely. The result was a disaster. The pillar exploded so violently that a huge piece of masonry shot across the churchyard and broke through the window of the upper floor of a bookshop where some women were working. Miraculously nobody was killed, but accounts for July–September 1672 list payments for repairs. The warning was heeded, and the Surveyor was instructed in no uncertain terms that gunpowder was not to be used again. The experiment was over and Wren was forced to return to using the ram.[13]

Wren had the walls of the nave taken down as far as the windows but then halted so that all energies could be concentrated on the east end. By July 1675 enough had been cleared for work to begin on the foundations. Wren and his officers began to mark out the new cathedral and to set about the rebuilding. The centre of all these operations was the new office of works.

6

LIFE IN THE OFFICE OF WORKS

The records of St Paul's provide the only description we have of the decoration and furnishing of an architect's site office in the seventeenth century. An office of works had existed at St Paul's before 1666; at the time of the Great Fire the cathedral was undergoing a programme of repairs, and like most large buildings or institutions today the cathedral maintained a small permanent staff to look after the maintenance and repair of the fabric. It was this office that Wren would take charge of in 1668, expanding its staff and turning it into an efficient centre for controlling all aspects of the building operations.

The duties of the king's Commission for Rebuilding St Paul's and those of its officers were set down at a meeting held on 5 August 1675, although officers had already been appointed some time beforehand. There were three principal officers – the Surveyor (Wren), the Assistant Surveyor (Edward Woodroffe) and the Clerk of Works (John Tillison) – and one assistant officer, the Labourer of Trust. The latter was an office position, but the appointment was the responsibility of the Clerk of Works rather than the committee, and the pay (2s. a day) was recorded in the list of labourers' wages rather than those of office staff. The first Labourer of Trust was a man called Lawrence Spencer; he was twenty-eight years old in 1675, hardly young but probably still the youngest person in the office.[1]

The commission's building sub-committee had to approve the drafts of all contracts, which were drawn up by a Clerk of Works. The Surveyor was responsible for writing warrants for the purchase of materials, which were recorded in a book kept for that purpose. The Assistant Surveyor received a salary of £100 per year; he not only stood in for the Surveyor in his absence, but also acted as the Purveyor. In this capacity he was responsible for sourcing all the building materials, for weighing and counting them as they came on site, and for keeping track of the stores. The Assistant Surveyor was also responsible for drawing up the monthly accounts. He would give the supplies he received to the Clerk of Works, who would check them against the accounts and enter them in his own book. In this way the Clerk and Purveyor could check on each other, and the Surveyor (by looking at his book of warrants and comparing it with that of the Clerk) could check on them both. In modern management parlance, there was a clear segregation of duties and a system of internal control. The Clerk of Works was responsible for the store's security and for issuing materials on site, helped in his duties by the Labourer of Trust. The Clerk also had to keep the monthly books, record the committee's minutes and act as the paymaster; for this work he received the same salary as the Assistant Surveyor and had lodgings in Convocation House Yard ('on the south side against the street').[2]

How many of these officers were actually present at St Paul's on any particular day is an interesting question. John Tillison, the Clerk of Works (not to be confused with John Tillotson, dean of St Paul's and later archbishop of Canterbury) was almost certainly there full time, but Woodroffe was also surveyor for Westminster Abbey and must occasionally have had to attend to his duties there. From 1669 they were joined by John Oliver, who oversaw the construction of the Deanery. When Woodroffe died in December 1675, it was Oliver who replaced him as Assistant Surveyor and he remained in that position until his death in 1701, when he in turn was replaced by Thomas Bateman. But Oliver, like

Woodroffe, had considerable responsibilities elsewhere, both with Wren in the City Church office and in his position as Master Mason of the King's Works (1686–1701).[3]

When Tillison died in 1685, his role of Clerk of Works was split between two people: his long-time assistant Lawrence Spencer (who now took the title Clerk of Works), and Thomas Russell, who occupied the new position of Clerk of the Cheque. The latter post was essentially the role of Paymaster: previously it had been listed among the duties of the Clerk of Works, but may have been delegated to Lawrence Spencer.[4]

John Scarborrow joined the office from 1688, helping John Oliver by acting as 'measurer'. He was replaced in 1696 by William Dickinson, who appears to have been an able architect in his own right. Drawings in his hand for the west end of the cathedral appear from 1701 onwards. There was only one officially appointed draughtsman, Nicholas Hawksmoor. He first appears in the accounts in 1690/91, but it is likely that he had been working on drawings for the rebuilding of St Paul's at least five years before that date. Various other craftsmen also helped in this respect: Edward Pearce, for instance, is known to have prepared a number of the early drawings for the cathedral, but whether he produced them in the office is unclear.[5]

In addition to these named individuals were the servants and clerks they employed, who rarely appear in accounts because they were not paid directly by the cathedral. It is not clear how many servants there were. We know, for example, that a Mr Henry Wood worked for a long time as John Oliver's assistant because the cathedral agreed to continue to employ him after his master's death in 1701, but we have no idea of when his employment started or whether he was one of many.[6]

Before the Great Fire, the cathedral office of works had been based at the sign of the Saracen's Head, in St Paul's Churchyard. These rooms were furnished with ten chairs, a table and a carpet. In the days before street numbers, all buildings carried signs that hung above the door.

Sometimes these signs represented a particular trade that was carried out in the building, but often they were emblems that may once have had a significance at some stage in the building's history, but which been adopted unchanged by new inhabitants. Thus the Saracen's Head was not necessarily a tavern as we might suppose today: it was probably just a house with that particular sign above the door. It presumably burned down in the Fire, because in October 1666 work began on a new set of offices in Convocation House Yard.[7]

By the turn of the seventeenth century the Convocation House – the original octagonal chapter house of the cathedral – had fallen into disrepair. In the 1660s only an empty shell remained in the centre of the yard, both the floor and the roof having fallen in. In the Middle Ages it had been surrounded by a magnificent two-storey cloister, but this seems to have collapsed completely in the Fire, leaving only the foundations of the pillars and the outer walls. These outer walls had been preserved because people had built houses up against them on the sides facing the street. There was a passage to the west – between the yard and St Gregory's Church – that gave access to a door in the south side of the cathedral. Since the works disrupted the flow of traffic around the cathedral, the commission decided to leave this passage open as a public right of way. A fenced-off lane was built right across the remains of the old nave so that the public could pass between the south and the north doors through the middle of the cathedral building site.

Convocation House Yard now became the centre of operations, chiefly because it was easy to secure. Here, all records, drawings, models and expensive building materials were stored under lock and key, and guarded by two mastiff dogs kept by the Clerk of Works.[8] The new office was built to a height of two storeys on the west side of the yard between October 1666 and March 1667. The lower rooms were used as stores and living quarters, while the upper rooms housed the offices for drawing and administration.[9]

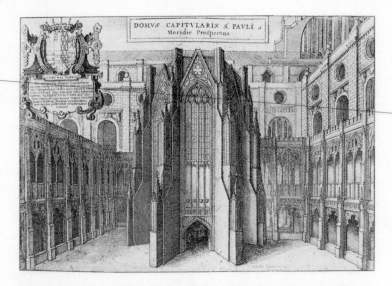

The Convocation House (Chapter House) of the old cathedral and the two-storey cloister that surrounded it. After the Fire, the office of works was built in the remains of the cloister. The Great Model was displayed in the Chapter House itself.

Payments for furnishings give us some idea of what the office of works must have looked like. The main room on the first floor was hung with green baize, and it had wide wooden floorboards that were painted black and matching skirting boards. In the centre of the room was a long table surrounded by seven chairs, and around the walls were cupboards for storing drawings and accounts, and tables for working at and laying out drawings. Since the whole building was almost certainly set on the old cloister foundations, the upper room was probably only about 10 feet (3 m) wide, but it may have been up to 30 or 40 feet (9 to 12 m) long. It was lit by iron casement windows, and there is some suggestion that it may have had rooflights. To be useful for drawing the room was presumably tall enough for the windows to let in a reasonable amount of light, and down its length there were a number of fireplaces to provide warmth in winter. We know that the whole complex, including the Clerk of Works' lodgings and the Surveyor's Office, had eleven fireplaces because they were included in the hearth-tax returns in March 1678.[10]

It was here in the upper room that the officers of works kept the accounts and oversaw the design and construction of the cathedral. The same room was probably used also for meetings of the sub-committee of the commissioners and for weekly meetings with the various master craftsmen. In 1668 three rooms were added to the office for the storage of the cathedral archives. These were not the records of the building works (which were kept in a locked cupboard in the office itself) but the ancient records and manuscripts of the cathedral that would eventually be moved to the library. In 1673 the old Convocation House in the middle of the yard was reroofed and converted into a room to house the Great Model, which was constructed there and which stayed there until the building works necessitated its move inside the cathedral itself.[11]

Wren's regular attendance on site appears to have started only in early 1672, in anticipation of which he added two more rooms to the office in December 1671: one for himself and one for the storage of models. The position of these rooms in relation to the main office is unclear, but it is highly likely that Wren's office was on the first floor, with a connecting door to the main room. It seems to have been a timber-framed structure and internally it was quite lavish. The walls were panelled rather than hung with baize, and the Surveyor had it fitted out with his own drawing table and cupboards. The windows were furnished with curtains, and there was a map of London hanging over the wooden mantelpiece. It was from this room that Wren oversaw the works until, in due course, the office of works was dismantled to make way for the nave of the new cathedral and moved to a more temporary structure nearby. The whole design operation was now based at St Paul's, with Wren in regular attendance whenever his other commitments allowed.[12]

Although there is a house in Cardinal's Wharf on the south side of the Thames that carries a plaque claiming that Wren lived there when he was building St Paul's, we know that this was not the case.[13] Wren's appointment as Surveyor of the King's Works in 1669 had given him a very substantial house in the Palace of Whitehall, where he lived. This house overlooked Scotland Yard, the centre of operations for the whole of the King's Works, which contained houses for the other officers and areas for storing materials. The house itself has long since disappeared, but was located north of the Banqueting House on Whitehall. In 1670 Wren was also appointed to oversee the design and reconstruction of the City churches. The drawing offices for the City churches and for the Royal Works appear to have been in (or attached to) his house in Whitehall. Much of Wren's time would have been spent here, particularly during the period 1670–75 when most of the churches were under construction. He still held his professorship in Oxford, where he had a set of rooms in All Souls (he resigned only in 1673), but it seems likely that he was neglecting his university duties from 1670 onwards in favour of his growing commitments in London.

Wren's house and office in Whitehall were about 1½ miles (2.5 km) from St Paul's. Today it would take about half an hour to walk between the two, but it would probably have taken slightly longer through the busy, narrow, pitted and muddy streets of seventeenth-century London. River transport was more common in Wren's day: ferrymen plied the river looking for trade and Wren may have gone to and from the City by boat. He would have had much to attend to there, and it was a journey that he could easily make every day without it taking him away from Whitehall for too long.

We cannot reconstruct Wren's daily movements in any detail. What we do know is that it eventually became his habit to go to the cathedral on Saturdays to meet his chief craftsmen – something he did every week for thirty-five years. He also had to attend meetings of the commissioners' sub-committees. Officially, these weekly meetings were scheduled for 2 o'clock every Thursday afternoon, but in practice they were held less frequently, and the day of the week changed to suit the individual members' busy diaries. As Wren could not be on site most of the time, much of the work had to be overseen by his office of works.[14]

It is important to understand that the office of works was not primarily a drawing office. Its main function was to manage the flow of money and materials in and out of the site and to monitor the progress of works. These were difficult tasks that left little time for drawing, but then the construction of St Paul's relied less on drawings than a modern building project.

The drawings and plans were drafted on boards fabricated on request by the carpenters. They were not the freestanding pieces of furniture that later became common, but merely smoothed and strengthened wooden surfaces that were either propped up on tables or used flat. Wren's contemporary Roger Pratt suggested that an architect should start the drawing process by finding the largest possible piece of parchment, vellum or paper. Parchment was made out of sheepskin that had been scraped and whitened with chalk. Before the arrival of paper it had commonly been used for making books: it was stable and long-lasting, but it was expensive. At St Paul's all the drawings were done on paper.[15]

Paper was not commonly used in Europe until the eleventh century. It was laboriously made by hand and was available in a range of sizes whose names (foolscap, Royal, Imperial) remain in use today. The size of the frame in which the paper was made determined the size of the paper. Some draughtsmen habitually cut off the rough edges with which the paper was supplied (for instance Thomas Laine, who worked on the City churches), while others (like Wren himself) usually left them on. The paper usually carried a watermark, which in the late seventeenth century revealed the place but not the date of manufacture. The paper for St Paul's displayed a crown watermark and came mostly from merchants in Holland, which was a major centre for the paper trade during this period.[16]

The large sheet of paper was fixed to the board with pins or wax. The next step was to determine the scale to be used. Today, plans are generally produced to certain fixed scales that appear on standard mass-produced scale rules, so that the reader of the drawing can quickly read off dimensions. In the seventeenth century, dimensions would be calculated using dividers, which would be set according to the scale bar drawn for that purpose and then used to extrapolate real measurements from the drawing itself. This meant that in theory any scale could be used, although in practice scales of 4, 5, 6 and 10 feet to the inch seem to have been preferred.[17]

The drawing work proper could now begin. If the drawing was to be copied from another, the outlines of the original were pricked though with a needle onto a new sheet, the dots then joined in pencil and finished in ink. When producing a completely new drawing, the draughtsman could use ink from the start, but (then as now) it was more common to begin by creating an underdrawing. This might be done by scoring the paper with a fine metal point or with a lead pencil, according to the draughtsman's preference. Lead pencils were a comparatively new invention, graphite first being used for drawing in the late sixteenth century. Once the underdrawing was complete, coloured washes were applied. Drawings from this period have been reproduced so many times in black and white it is easy to forget that they were often coloured, with different hues being used to represent different materials. The outlines were finally gone over carefully in ink.[18]

The ink lines of surviving architectural drawings are often brown, but this was not intentional. The main ingredients of the black ink used at the end of the seventeenth century were iron sulphate (then known as 'copperas'), oak galls (parasitic growths on trees), water and wine. The ink's iron content rusted, and poorly made ink degraded more. Thus the sepia lines seen in old architectural drawings are simply black ink that has turned brown with age.[19] Ready-made ink is known to have been purchased from local stationers for use at St Paul's, but it was probably used only for writing. It has been inferred from differences in the inks on surviving drawings that the draughtsmen preferred to make their own.

In the eighteenth century, architectural draughtsmen usually employed steel ruling pens. The nib consisted of two metal blades, the spacing of which determined the thickness of the line being drawn. Already in the seventeenth century sets were being produced that included ruling pens, compasses and dividers. Examination of the drawings suggests that Wren and his draughtsmen also used traditional quill pens made from crow or goose feathers (crow feathers were apparently preferred because they were stronger). Such quills did not last long so a continual supply was required, and in September 1690 the office ordered 600 at a total cost of 6*s*. They had to be carefully cut to shape with a specially designed knife (the origin of the term 'penknife'); Wren's is preserved at St Paul's. Other drafting implements – such as set squares – were made by the joiners on site.[20]

A large number of drawings survive for St Paul's: there are 68 in the collection of All Souls College, Oxford, and 220 that remained in the cathedral are now stored in the Guildhall Library in London. The All Souls collection appears mostly to consist of early designs, which probably come from Wren's Whitehall office and may well have been drawn there. Those from St Paul's now stored in the Guildhall relate more closely to the final project, although it is noticeable how few of the surviving drawings actually show the cathedral as built.[21]

The building works at St Paul's were divided into separate sections and then by trade. Each team of craftsmen worked on a section and was paid either by the day or according to the amount they built. In terms of information relating to the overall design, all they needed were daily instructions for the piece of work they were engaged on and a steady supply of materials. In most cases an oral command would do, and many queries could have been (and no doubt were) answered that way. The building accounts are full of entries for templates – profiles traced onto wood by Wren, one of the draughtsmen or the Clerk of Works, and cut out and strengthened by joiners. These were provided for the cutting of stonework. Once the stones had been cut, they were set out on full-size tracing floors. There were a number of these (presumably one for each team) around the site. As each block was cut, it could thus be compared both to the template and to its neighbours laid out on the tracing floor before being lifted into position for final fitting. None of this required a single paper drawing. The drawings that were produced were probably for presentation or coordination drawings intended for the design team rather than for the craftsmen; the latter type enabled the architects to test out ideas at an early stage, to ensure that parts would fit together, and to make certain that sections would be transferred accurately onto the tracing floors.[22]

Models played a much greater role in the design of St Paul's than is generally realized. In *Parentalia*, Wren's son had stated that after the rejection of the Great Model, his father had declared that he would never build another model again. This statement has tended to be taken at face value, but an examination of the accounts reveals that during the course of the works Wren in fact constructed over seventy models for St Paul's (the exact number is impossible to determine because in this period the word 'model' was also used for a design). The models varied in size and complexity, ranging from simple full-scale mock-ups of parts of the cornices to large-scale structural models of the dome executed in stone.[23]

All these items – drawings, templates, models – were created in the office of works, which for over thirty years was at the heart of the building operation. But in 1675, many years before these working practices became established, Wren and his colleagues faced their first major problem: how to construct the cathedral's foundations. Their decision turned out to have far-reaching consequences for the design of the whole building.

7

THE PHOENIX RISING

If you stand outside the south transept of St Paul's today and look up, you will see, carved in the pediment high above you, a phoenix with out-stretched wings rising from a fire, below which a single word has been engraved. The phoenix is of course a mythological bird that was believed to rise magically from the ashes – a clear allusion to the new cathedral being born out of the Great Fire. Yet the inscription alludes to a strange event that occurred during the setting out of the foundations, before a single stone had been laid. It is said that when Wren began the rebuilding he started by marking out the dome on the ground. He realized that he needed a stone to mark the exact centre of the dome. Not wishing to leave the spot, he called for a labourer to bring him the first stone that came to hand. Without looking, the man picked up a suitably sized piece and did as he was asked. When Wren turned it over, he discovered that it was part of a gravestone bearing only a single word of an inscription: 'RESURGAM' ('I shall rise again'). There could hardly have been a more auspicious beginning.[1]

There is some disagreement about the date on which the first stone of the cathedral was laid. John Ward's *Lives of the Gresham Professors* records that it happened on 21 June 1675 at the south-east corner of the building. Edward Strong's account, written in 1716, corresponds, adding that the first stone was laid by Thomas Strong (the author's elder brother). Elias Ashmole's diary entry for 25 June reads: '6:30am The Foundation of St Paul's Church, laid', while the antiquarian Anthony Wood noted in his diary that it is 'said' to have happened on 28 June. It has even been stated that Charles II laid the first stone, but this seems unlikely given the general confusion surrounding the date. It was probably a low-key event involving only a few building workers and perhaps the dean and some other clergy. As far as the building works were concerned, it mattered little. The primary concern was what followed: the laying of the foundations.[2]

The pediment above the portico of the south transept.

Parentalia alleges that Wren 'began to lay the foundations in the west-end and … proceeded successfully through the Dome to the east end', but this is just one of many questionable statements in the book. Wren's son Christopher, who almost certainly wrote this account, was born in 1675 and for this early period must have relied entirely on stories told to him many years later by his father and others. The building accounts are clear, however: the foundations were started at the east end and worked westwards. It could not have been otherwise, because much of the west end of the old cathedral – including its foundations – were not demolished until the middle of the 1680s. Only at the east end was the site clear and excavated, ready for work to begin.[3]

Parentalia also contains an account of how, when digging the foundations in the north-east 'Angle', workmen found that the ground was loose and that they could not dig down to anything more stable. Wren's solution was typically pragmatic: he is said to have dug deeper before building an arch over the soft ground. Despite surveys of the foundations carried out by Mervyn Macartney, the cathedral surveyor, in 1914, nothing of this sort has been found. He was, however, able to show that most of cathedral's foundations are very shallow, extending only a few feet below the floor of the crypt.[4]

Today, soil mechanics and geotechnical engineering provide us with a much greater understanding of foundation design. In the seventeenth century Wren could do little more than rely on established practice and on his own intuition. At that time, a number of different foundations were employed according to the perceived bearing capacity of the soil. The simplest, used for foundations on firm ground, consisted of nothing more than stepping out the wall beneath ground level. Rows of columns posed a particular problem since they concentrated load; the solution Wren devised for his library at Trinity College, Cambridge, was to build a set of inverted arches underground to link the columns. This method was not new: it had been advocated by Alberti in his *Ten Books on Architecture*, published in 1486. On uneven ground a timber raft was often constructed under the masonry walls – a method Wren employed on a number of his City churches. Finally, on very soft ground timber piles were used.[5]

Most buildings had very shallow foundations that extending only a few feet below the lowest floor level. Ideas about good bearing materials were rudimentary and often based on myth rather than fact. However, long experience had shown that in the first few years of construction, buildings could move quite dramatically as the weight compressed the soil beneath. It was thus common to spread building work over a number of years so as to take this settlement into account, and it was understood that building too fast could lead to disaster. In general, it did not matter if a building sank uniformly on its foundations into the earth, but problems did arise where one part of the structure sank more than the others, either because it weighed more (or, to be more accurate, applied more pressure on the ground) or because the subsoil at that point was weaker. This phenomenon is called differential settlement. The designers of St Paul's were aware of the problem and took a number of steps to try to avoid it. The first was to make sure that the new cathedral avoided the foundations of the old.

With his City churches, Wren generally built the new buildings directly on the existing foundations. The advantage of this strategy was that the ground had already been compressed, but of course it meant that the shape of each new building was limited by what had gone before. At St Paul's Wren tried to avoid building on the old foundations wherever possible. To do so he rotated the axis of his design so that the setting-out of the piers and walls bore no relation to the old groundplan. As *Parentalia* explains,

> To have built on the old Foundations must have confined
> the Surveyor too much to the old Plan and Form; the
> ruinous Walls in no Part were to be trusted again, nor

would old and new Work firmly unite, or stand together
without Cracks.[6]

At certain points the new walls inevitably crossed the lines of the old,
but Wren resisted the temptation simply to incorporate the existing foundations, instead breaking them up laboriously. His new cathedral had
much thicker walls and much larger piers, and he clearly understood that
reusing the existing work might later have given rise to problems of differential settlement.

Wren never recorded how he chose the orientation of the new cathedral, but since he was an able astronomer we can presume that his
solution was not entirely arbitrary: indeed, recent calculations have suggested that the building's main axis might have been aligned with sunrise
on Easter Sunday 1675.[7]

Having determined that the new cathedral should not lie over the
old, Wren investigated ground conditions by digging pits around the site.
He discovered that beneath soil level the natural ground was composed of
'potter's clay' (also called brickearth) over sands and gravel over more
clay. Water lay on the top of the clay, beneath the sand and the gravel.
A decision was made to form the foundations in the potter's clay, at a
depth of between 4 feet (1.2 m) and 7 feet 6 inches (2.3 m) below the floor
of the crypt. These foundations consist of nothing more than a stepping
out of the base of the walls.[8]

Wren clearly believed that the brickearth was stronger than the loose
sand and gravel layers below, but in this he was, as we shall see, pro-
foundly mistaken. Brickearth is an inconsistent material composed of
varying quantities of sand, clay and silt, which expands and contracts
with changes in moisture content and loading. If Wren had chosen to dig
his foundations slightly deeper, he could have founded the cathedral on
the layer of sand and gravel beneath, which would have provided a much
firmer base and led to less settlement. Sand and gravel might sound like

poor substances on which to construct a cathedral (anyone who has tried digging holes in sand knows how the sides cave in). However, when sand or gravel is confined on all sides, as it is in a deep excavation, it behaves differently, becoming relatively incompressible and in fact making a very stable base on which to build.

Wren's decision to found the building on brickearth led to problems within a few decades. The great piers that supported the dome began to settle even before they were completed, and as work progressed they continued to settle at a faster rate than the rest of the building. Not only was this a great cause for concern, but it led Wren to completely rethink the design of the upper parts of the cathedral and, most importantly, the structure of the dome.

While excavating for the foundations, the workmen unearthed various artefacts. *Parentalia* mentions that these included a great abundance of urns, sacrificial vessels and pottery ware. Wren and his colleagues were

Plan from the Wren office showing the orientation of the new cathedral in relation to the old, now thought to be inaccurate.

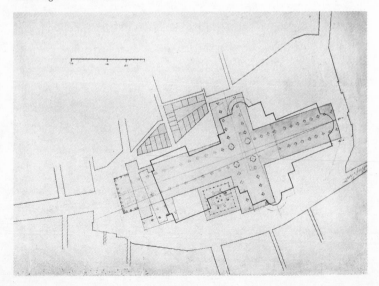

intrigued by the discoveries, and Wren gave several reports on them to the Royal Society. Today the Royal Society is dedicated wholly to science, but in Wren's day the interests of its members covered virtually every sphere of knowledge, including antiquarianism, the forerunner of modern archaeology. Wren made no attempt to record his findings systematically, but he took some satisfaction in refuting the claims of previous historians that Old St Paul's had been built on the site of a Roman Temple to Diana, noting that no remains of any such structure had been found, nor were there any ox skulls, antlers or boar tusks that might have supported the hypothesis. These brief excursions into archaeology were no doubt a welcome relief from the day-to-day problems faced by those on site as the work progressed, the greatest of which were financial.[9]

8

FINANCING THE WORKS

St Paul's Cathedral required a massive sum of money to build. The final entry in the accounts calculated that by 1716 it had cost £804,758. The amount passing through the accounts, including loans taken out to cover expenses and later repaid, was over £1.1 million. It is very difficult to provide an accurate conversion, but this figure could probably be multiplied one thousand times to give an equivalent in today's currency. It was by far the most expensive building constructed in England during this period.[1]

Money always had been a problem at St Paul's. It had been a problem before the Great Fire and was even more so afterwards. This situation manifested itself most obviously in delay. The Great Fire had destroyed the old cathedral in 1666, but the ceremony of laying the foundation stone did not take place until June 1675 – a gap of nine years. A late start may have suited Wren, who was at his busiest during these years working on the City churches and who would have found it difficult to devote himself entirely to St Paul's. In any case, in the immediate aftermath of the Fire both building workers and materials were in short supply as all available resources were engaged in rebuilding the City. It was most likely clear from the outset that any work on the new cathedral would be delayed until much of the reconstruction elsewhere was complete. This would also have allowed time to clear the site, demolish the choir, dig up the crypt and generally prepare the ground. However, a further reason for delay was uncertainty over finance. Eventually it became apparent that if work on the cathedral was to begin at all, it must do so without all the money in place. Thus, even as the first stone was being laid, it was unclear how enough money would be found to pay for the building. It was a massive act of faith on everyone's part.

St Paul's was constructed under the reign of six monarchs:

Charles II (1660–85)

James II (1685–88)

William III (1688–1702) and Mary II (1688–94)

Anne (1702–14)

George I (1714–27)

Wren's relationship with Charles II could hardly have been better: he had been appointed through the king's direct intervention. Charles II was a driving force in the early stages of the project, which he saw as symbolizing the restoration of the monarchy. As a serial philanderer who was profligate with money, the king was continually in debt. His inability to help finance the cathedral works hindered the project considerably at the outset, but his continued interest certainly helped in raising money from elsewhere. His brother James II had never expected to be king, and thus had moved more widely outside court circles. He had regularly attended the Royal Society and knew Wren better than Charles had. Moreover, he was if anything even more enthusiastic about St Paul's than his elder brother. Unfortunately his reign was beset by political problems and was cut short by the Glorious Revolution of 1688. The transitionary period between 1689 and 1690 saw work grind to a halt and disturbing changes in the Church hierarchy for Wren, but it was soon clear that rebuilding could continue much as before thanks to the enthusiastic support of Mary. William, however, was engaged in long and costly wars with France and took little interest in the cathedral; his wife's death in 1694 was thus a significant setback. In 1702 William died and was succeeded by Anne, who proved a most enthusiastic supporter of St Paul's and particularly of Wren, stepping in to help the aged Surveyor in time of need during the last stages of construction. It was under Anne's aegis that the taxes that ensured the cathedral's completion were raised. Although George I of Hanover did not reverse the taxes, he did (as we shall see) allow Wren's enemies to move against him once more.

The Commission for Rebuilding St Paul's that Charles II created on 12 November 1673 – and which replaced the body entrusted with the task repairing the old cathedral – had wide-ranging powers to demolish and rebuild as they saw fit and to raise the capital to do so. Its one hundred initial members consisted of major post-holders at court, from the Lord Chancellor downwards, most of whom never attended meetings. Only six members (including both the dean and the bishop of London) had to be present for a meeting to be quorate. The first meeting took place at Lambeth Palace on Monday 11 May 1674, with 47 people in attendance. This was to be the highest turnout: thereafter there were rarely more than 20 members present, and on a day-to-day basis the commission delegated its powers to a smaller sub-committee consisting only of those most interested in the work – chiefly the archbishop of Canterbury, the bishop of London, the dean and the cathedral's residentary canons. Most meetings of this sub-committee consisted of no more than 14 people.[2]

Most of the archbishops of Canterbury presiding during the period of construction were not only known to Wren, but had also been actively involved in St Paul's before their promotions. Their names were:

Gilbert Sheldon (1663–77)

William Sancroft (1677–90)

John Tillotson (1690–94)

Thomas Tenison (1694–1715)

Of the four, Sheldon and Sancroft had been involved in Wren's initial appointment, while Tillotson had worked closely with him as dean and was a personal friend. As Bishop of Lincoln and a member of the commission, Tenison had been an enthusiastic supporter of the cathedral even before his appointment, and he regularly attended meetings. He was to play a particularly important role in the financial crisis of 1696–97, when the cathedral ran out of money and it seemed as if work might have to stop altogether.

Throughout the works there were only four bishops of London:

Gilbert Sheldon (1660–63)

Humphrey Henchman (1663–75)

Henry Compton (1675–1713)

John Robinson (1714–23)

Humphrey Henchman, who was seventy-one when he took over from Gilbert Sheldon in 1663, appears to have been amiable and content to attend the commission meetings without making much of an active contribution. He did, however, donate generously to the building fund during his lifetime, and when he died in October 1675 he left a considerable sum towards the works in his will. His successor was one of Wren's close friends, Henry Compton. The Surveyor and the bishop had been contemporaries at Oxford and had travelled together in France. Compton was to play a key role in raising funds in the early years and supported Wren throughout the works, although he became too frail and senile in his old age to help the architect in his later battles with Henry Godolphin. By the time Robinson was appointed, work was almost complete.

The building sub-committee of the commission was headed by the dean, whose support was essential. During the period 1660–1726 Wren worked under five separate deans:

William Sancroft (1665–77)

John Stillingfleet (1677–88)

John Tillotson (1688–90)

William Sherlock (1691–1707)

Henry Godolphin (1707–26)

Sancroft had been instrumental in Wren's appointment. The two worked well together, and it was said to be with some regret that Sancroft left St Paul's to become archbishop of Canterbury. His new position still allowed him to take a keen interest in the cathedral, however, and he made a point of attending every meeting of the commission until he resigned in 1690. Stillingfleet, Sancroft's successor as dean, is thought to have been one of the figures who objected to the Great Model design. This must have made early relations somewhat strained, but Stillingfleet was an capable administrator and appears to have become a great supporter of Wren, even asking him to rebuild his church, St Andrew Holborn. His successor, John Tillotson, had been on the building committee as a residentiary of St Paul's and was a member of the Royal Society. When Sancroft resigned as archbishop of Canterbury in 1690, it was Tillotson who was elevated to succeed him, once again assuring support from that high office. William Sherlock who replaced him as dean was an able, if controversial, figure, but he seems to have been content to let the Surveyor work without interference. It was thus only with the appointment of Godolphin, as we shall see, that Wren met with determined resistance and indeed open hostility.

The money for the new St Paul's came from two sources. The first was gifts elicited by the commission. For the first thirteen years, from 1675 until 1688, donations made up half of the total amount raised (about £3,000 a year), but thereafter these began to tail off dramatically. By the beginning of the eighteenth century only £1 a year came in from gifts. There were two reasons for this decline. The first was that initial enthusiasm for the project inevitably began to wane as the decades went by and still the cathedral remained unfinished. The second reason was that from 1685 subscribers had the option of lending the cathedral money and receiving interest in return – an option that undoubtedly made free gifts less appealing.[3]

The second source of income (and by far the most important from 1688 onwards) was the Coal Tax and the loans that could be raised

Date started	Date due to end	Rate per chaldron*	Av. income per year	Total raised
May 1670	Sept. 1687	$4\frac{1}{2}d.$	£5,000	£84,355
Oct. 1687	March 1700	$14\frac{2}{5}d.$	£19,000	£247,674
Oct. 1700	Oct. 1716	$7\frac{1}{2}d.$	£11,500	£183,990
15 May 1708	15 May 1716	+ 2s.	£36,500	£294,161

* A chaldron was the equivalent of 16 sacks.

Table showing the rates of Coal Tax due to St Paul's and the total amounts raised.

against it. Throughout the Middle Ages wood had been the main fuel for both warmth and for cooking, but coal began to replace it for domestic heating from the sixteenth century onwards.[4]

Coal's greater efficiency give it obvious advantages over wood, but the main drawback was the smoke it produced. Coal smoke was far more polluting: the dark, oily soot clung to walls and furniture and is said to have been one of the reasons why easy-to-clean timber panelling replaced hangings in well-to-do households. Worse still, burning coal led to sulphurous smogs. The problems of coal pollution in London had grown so bad by the end of seventeenth century that Wren's friend John Evelyn had written a book complaining about the fuel and campaigning for its abolition.[5]

Coal had been taxed since the Middle Ages, but in 1667 an additional levy had been added to help finance rebuilding after the Great Fire. Several years later the City of London lobbied for an increase – a provision that was ultimately incorporated in the Rebuilding of London Act of 1670. This included an allowance for St Paul's. One of the great advantages of raising revenue in this fashion was that the mechanism was already in place. The tax was already collected by the fifteen 'Coal Meters' who were responsible for measuring the fuel as it was unloaded in the London docks. Great fleets of up to one hundred ships at a time set out from Newcastle, where it was mined, and sailed down the North Sea, delivering about half a million tons of coal a year to the city.[6]

Despite its obvious convenience, the tax proved less reliable than initially hoped. There were problems with collecting it, coal ships were sunk by enemy action – England was at war with the Dutch (1665–67 and 1672–74) and the French (1689–97 and 1702–13) – and the amount of coal consumed varied according to the season.[7]

Until 1687 the City administered the coal levy through the Chamberlain's Office and the process seems to have run relatively smoothly. When the City's entitlement came to an end, the Lords Commissioners appointed a Receiver, who had a staff of five clerks to oversee the deputies of the Coal Meters. A Comptroller was also appointed, who had to be sent duplicates of all receipts from the Coal Meters so that he could check the Receiver's accounts. The Receiver was William Middleton, who was also the cathedral solicitor, and the position of Comptroller was occupied by Colonel Pierce. The collection of the tax was obviously open to abuse: in 1690 Wren obtained permission to look into the books and it was found that they did not tally. Whether Middleton was taking a cut or was merely negligent is unclear, but he was dismissed and replaced on Wren's suggestion by Thomas Bateman. Colonel Pierce was initially kept on but later also dismissed.[8]

The Coal Tax in the early years was nowhere near enough to cover expenditure, and despite all the subscriptions, benefactions and collections, income in the early years continually fell short of what was required. To solve this problem Wren gradually began to pay his contractors later and later. The main accounts suggest that initially no more work was done than could be paid for, and that each workman was paid in the month the work was done or shortly thereafter. But careful examination of the Acquittance Books shows that by 1679 craftsmen were already being paid six months late, a delay that became longer and longer as the works progressed. By 1694 the commissioners owed £7,800 to various craftsmen who petitioned for assistance. They decided to pay them interest at the rate of 6 per cent a year. Records of subsequent interest payments reveal the amounts owed: by 1697 most craftsmen were each owed hundreds of pounds, and several were owed thousands. 'Borrowing' from the contractors in this way not surprisingly caused a certain amount of disquiet. In any event, it was a measure that could not solve the longer-term financial problems. The only solution was to ask for a further increase in the money granted to the cathedral from the Coal Tax. By the mid 1680s the City churches were nearing completion so it was possible to argue that a greater percentage could be devoted to St Paul's without raising the overall tax. Urgent action was required since the previous Act was due to expire in 1687. Unfortunately there was one major obstacle: the king.[9]

In 1681 Charles II had fallen out with Parliament over the Popish Plot affair and the resulting Exclusion Bill designed to keep the king's brother from the throne. Charles refused to recall Parliament, and without Parliament there could be no new Act. Money for the cathedral was on the point of running out altogether, and people began to speculate that it would never be completed. On 2 February 1685 Charles II was taken ill. Despite (or perhaps because of) the ministrations of his physicians, who tried every combination of cupping, bleeding and cauterizing that modern medicine of the time could offer, Charles died four days later. Completely unexpectedly, his brother James was now king: as well as the coronation, a general election was held and Parliament was recalled to settle matters of state. James II also had to renew the Commission for Rebuilding St Paul's.

When the Coal Tax came up for renewal, Wren moved to have himself elected to Parliament (in this case as a candidate for Devonshire Borough, Plympton St Maurice) so that he could argue the case himself in the House of Commons. Wren was successful, and in 1685 Parliament granted the cathedral 18*d*. per chaldron until October 1700. More importantly, St Paul's was permitted to borrow against the duty's security. This was essential since revisions to the revenue would not come into force for another two years, when the previous Act was due to expire. In the meantime, on the advice of their Surveyor, the commission took the opportunity to borrow £10,150 at an interest of 6 per cent per annum, a competitive market rate. With the money raised in this way it was possible to get work moving quickly, but the commissioners were careful and – to avoid crippling interest – had repaid most of their debts within three years.[10]

In 1694 a further crisis loomed. Building expenses increased as construction progressed and, with the tax due to expire in 1700, it was becoming increasingly difficult to persuade lenders to invest. In March 1697 the Whig government reluctantly voted to extend the tax from 1700 until October 1716 but only at a considerably reduced rate; they also penalized Wren by ordering that half his salary should be withheld until the cathedral was complete. The new tax rate was not enough and debts piled up – a situation remedied only upon the accession of Queen Anne, when the new Tory government voted that an additional 2*s*. should be directed to the cathedral, starting from May 1708. This move finally solved all the commissioners' financial problems and ensured the cathedral's completion. The change did not come into force immediately; but in the short term the cathedral could borrow against it, and when it did come into force the extra £35,000 a year quickly paid off all outstanding debts.[11]

Over the whole period between 1668 and 1716, the total raised or borrowed by the cathedral was a massive £1,157,782 10*s*. 2½*d*. The total money expended amounted to £1,095,556 1*s*. 4¾*d*. Of this, the actual building work cost only £721,552 7*s*. 7¼*d*. The rest was repayment of loans and interest on those loans. The cathedral commissioners had borrowed £62,100 in the first thirteen years in which they were allowed to do so (1685–98); they had been lent a further £7,700 in 1701–2; and they borrowed considerably more when the 2s. rate came into force (the total between 1702 and 1716 amounting to £211,040). Interest paid on loans over the whole period at 6 per cent amounted to £83,205 9s. 9½d., making the overall cost of the cathedral – excluding the costs of buying properties around the churchyard and other expenses – £804,758 7s. 6¾d. Clearly, the accuracy of the figures shown in the accounts is illusory, but they do give some idea of the amounts of money involved. Many of those who lent money to the cathedral were themselves involved in its construction (a result of the contractors' debts being converted into loans in 1697), but others no doubt simply thought that 6 per cent interest was a good return on their investment. Wren himself lent over £3,300 of his own money towards the works, and Hawksmoor invested £1,500. But loans such as these were only one way in which money could be made from the building of the cathedral. Many workers profited handsomely from their trades.[12]

9

THE WEALTH OF MASONS

Once the first stones of St Paul's had been laid in 1675, work on the walls proceeded swiftly, and by 1676 those of the crypt in the east end were complete in several areas and the masonry was beginning to appear above ground level. Had construction continued at this pace the walls of the choir might have been finished by the end of the decade.

The walls and piers of the new St Paul's were constructed in the traditional manner used on the great Gothic cathedrals, with a rubble core encased between outer layers of ashlar (smooth-cut stone). Cutting stone is expensive and time-consuming, and throughout history it has been general practice to use ashlar only on a building's visible faces. In all periods the space between the walls has normally been filled up with rubble bound together with mortar. In smaller seventeenth-century buildings the stone was sometimes supported on a solid brick wall, or else brick was used for the inner face instead of stone: since the internal walls would be panelled or plastered, the difference in material did not matter.

It may have been usual practice when constructing on a massive scale to use rubble infill between ashlar walls, but if it was badly done this method could lead to cracking and structural failure. Problems are caused chiefly by the settlement of the core and by the infill being poorly attached to the encasing walls. In his pre-Fire survey of the piers of medieval St Paul's in 1666, Wren had noted that the old walls contained 'nothing but a Core of small Rubbish-stone, and much Mortar, which easily crushes and yields to the Weight'.[1]

Wren was obliged to employ a similar form of construction for his new cathedral, since the alternatives (a wall of solid squared and dressed ashlar construction, or of solid brick faced with ashlar) would have been prohibitively slow and expensive. But he learnt from the faults of the old cathedral, taking care that the stones for the casing were massive, accurately shaped with thin joints, and of varying depths so that they might be well keyed into the core, thus reducing the risk of compaction.

Mortar for the walls was also chosen with care. At the time St Paul's was constructed, the basic ingredients for mortar were lime, sand and water (the same materials that, when mixed with animal hair, were used to make plaster). The mortar was 'non-hydraulic' (meaning it would not harden underwater) and it was also comparatively weak. Lime mortars require a long time to absorb carbon dioxide from the air and attain their full strength. Wren did, however, experiment with adding a number of pozzolanic materials to his mortars. Pozzolans – named after a place in Italy where Roman builders found a useful volcanic ash – are additives used to produce stronger, quicker-setting mortars and plasters. These improved mortars and plasters were used by Wren in such areas as the brickwork of the dome and the underside of the vaults.[2]

Perhaps the most important feature of the cathedral walls was not the way in which they were made but the variation in their thickness. The walls of late Gothic cathedrals typically were constructed to be as thin as possible and needed to be stabilized by regular buttresses. Wren had rejected this arrangement, which would not have produced the Classical elevations he desired. Instead, both the Great Model and the Warrant designs featured thick walls interrupted by huge niches on the internal faces between the piers at floor level. In the cathedral as built, the external walls between the church floor and the triforium level are two and a half times as thick, over a similar height, as the equivalent walls in the old cathedral (see illustration on p. 110), meaning that no external buttressing was required.

From the outset Wren was conscious of the importance of choosing the correct masons for the job. In the Middle Ages, a single mason would have been in charge of the site and also responsible for much of the design. The appearance of the architect as a profession had changed matters, although for most projects a single mason was still appointed to oversee the works. This was not the case at St Paul's. Instead, the cathedral was divided up between a number of teams of masons who each worked on a separate section, each team effectively in competition with the others to finish the task as quickly as possible. It was an unusual arrangement, but mason-contractors in the seventeenth century were relatively small operators, and no single contractor could have afforded the financial risk of contracting for the whole of St Paul's.

In a letter of 1681 to the bishop of Oxford concerning the construction of Tom Tower in that city, Wren described the three methods of contracting current in the seventeenth century: 'By Day', 'By Measure' and 'By Great'. The first method, 'by day', had been commonly used throughout the Middle Ages to build castles, cathedrals, etc. Each workman was paid by the number of days he spent on site each month. This method allowed for great flexibility during construction and ensured that there were always enough workers on site, but there was little incentive for the men to complete their work quickly. In choosing to be paid 'by measure', a contractor undertook to carry out the work at an agreed rate for every yard of stone laid or similar unit. An appointed independent inspector called a 'measurer' would periodically visit the site and certify that a certain amount of work had been carried out, for which the contractor would then be paid. In this respect measurers were the forerunners of the modern quantity surveyor. The contractor who worked under this type of agreement had to have the financial wherewithal to pay his workmen between inspections; but he also had a strong incentive to work quickly, and the measuring process allowed for some checking of quality. The final method was 'by great' or 'by task', where the contractor undertook to do a piece of work (a wall or a house, for instance) for an agreed lump sum. This method carried the greatest risk for the contractor and relied on complicated checks and balances to prevent the contractor from cutting corners. For St Paul's Wren chose to pay his masons 'by measure', and it seems to have been very lucrative for them.[3]

In the early years of construction two teams of masons were in operation, one led by Joshua Marshall and the other by Thomas Strong. On Marshall's death in 1678, his contract was divided and taken over by Edward Pearce and Jasper Latham, while a further contract went to Thomas Wise, making four teams in total. Two more – one led by John Tompson and the other by Samuel Fulkes – were added in 1687. The sequence of contracts thereafter becomes increasingly complicated and is more easily understood as a diagram (see p. 74).[4]

Wren's contractors needed to be able to put enough men on the job to ensure that the work would be carried out satisfactorily. They also needed to be able pay those men on a regular basis, even if the contractor himself had to wait for his money. Although the work was measured twice a year, and the amounts due were agreed and entered into the accounts, it often took years to receive payment. In the meantime contractors were obliged to rely on their own financial resources or to borrow from colleagues. When they did finally receive their payment, mason-contractors expected to make a healthy profit and some of them become very rich indeed.

Joshua Marshall (1629–78) was one of the most successful. He came from a family of prominent masons: his father, Edward Marshall, had been Master of the Masons' Livery Company (1650) and Master Mason of the King's Works (1660–73), resigning his position so that his son could take over. Before the Great Fire, Joshua Marshall seems to have been a statuary mason, employed chiefly in sculpting monuments and elaborate

EAST END AND DOME

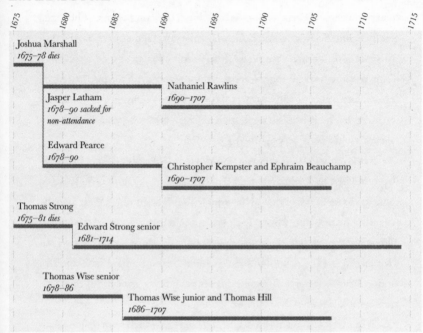

WEST END

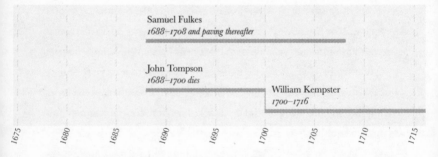

Table showing the succession of masons' contracts at St Paul's.

chimneypieces. After the Fire he shifted his activities to building, and in the following decade he took contracts worth over £46,000. But it is his personal wealth that is particularly noteworthy: upon his death he left over £10,000, which put him among the richest men in London (see table overleaf).[5] The mason-contractors at St Paul's fell into three groups: quarry-owners, statuary masons and building contractors. The first group included Thomas and Edward Strong and Christopher Kempster. The career of Thomas Strong (*c.* 1634–81) is in some respects typical for his profession: he had come from a prominent family of masons/quarry-owners and seems to have been a shrewd businessman. He first worked for Wren on his new block for Trinity College, Oxford, but following the Great Fire he saw fresh opportunities in London and moved there.[6]

As a young mason, Strong would have been obliged to join the Masons' Company in London, since all masons working in the City were required to be members of a City Livery Company (Guild). This system was the norm for all trades: each guild was in turn granted a charter allowing it to regulate the trade in question. There were three ways to join such a guild: by apprenticeship, by patrimony or by redemption. Apprentices paid for the privilege of working for a member of the guild for a period of seven or eight years, after which, if they were judged to have reached sufficient competence, they were granted their 'freedom' to join a guild and work in the City. Sons of guildsmen could claim their freedom ('by patrimony') without having to go through a formal apprenticeship. Lastly, those who were rich enough could simply pay a fee and join a guild ('by redemption'). However, to encourage workmen to help in reconstruction after the Fire, the Rebuilding of London Act of 1670 had allowed anyone to work in the City for a period of seven years without joining a guild, and any who did so were to be given their freedom of the City at the end that period.[7]

Thomas Strong joined the Masons' Company in 1670, paying by redemption to avoid having to wait seven years for his freedom. From his new London base, he became involved with Wren in the building of three City churches and the new St Paul's (it was Thomas who laid the first stone), and he no doubt he also worked elsewhere. But despite Strong's growing prosperity he never married, and when he died in his forties

Status	Fortune
Considerable fortune	£20,000
Rich	£10,000–20,000
Substantial merchants	£5,000–10,000
Middle-range merchants	£1,000–5,000
Prosperous tradesmen	£500–1,000
Artisans and petty retailers	under £500

Table showing differing degrees of personal wealth in the seventeenth century.[8]

in 1681, he left everything to his younger brother Edward (1652–1724) (Plate 2). Edward Strong thus inherited Thomas's quarries at Little Barrington and Taynton in Oxfordshire, together with his brother's properties and valuable contracts at St Paul's. He had been apprenticed to his elder brother when he was nineteen years old and no doubt had come to London to assist him. Edward was to become one of the most prominent masons of the age, taking his freedom of the Masons' Company in 1680, and becoming a warden in 1694 and its Master in 1696. His contracts for Wren's City churches and St Paul's were worth over £11,000, and Edward also worked on Winchester Palace, Morden Hospital, Greenwich Hospital and Blenheim Palace. He married the sister of Ephraim Beauchamp, another mason working at St Paul's. Edward's wealth was such that in later years he established himself as a landowner, buying two manors near St Albans in Hertfordshire. He died at the age of seventy-one on 8 February 1724, a year after Wren, having lived to see St Paul's completed and his son, also called Edward (1676–1741), take over the family business.[9]

Christopher Kempster (1627–1715) was also a mason and quarry-owner whose story in some ways mirrors that of Thomas Strong. He owned a quarry in Burford near Oxford and was sending stone to

London as early as 1668. Like Strong, he bought his freedom of the City by redemption in 1670, and he went on to become Master of the Masons' Company not once but twice (in 1691 and 1700). His first London building contract was with Strong on St Stephen's Walbrook, but thereafter he began working on a number of City churches as a contractor in his own right. Other projects Kempster worked during this period were Abingdon Town Hall and Winchester Palace. Wren had a high opinion of him, calling him 'a very able man, modest, honest and treatable. I have used him on good works ... and I can rely on him.' He died at the age of eighty-eight in 1715 and left his quarry to his youngest son, John, while his third son, William, finished off his contracts at St Paul's.[10]

Joshua Marshall, Edward Pearce and Jasper Latham were all statuary masons. Pearce (c. 1630–95), a brilliant carver, probably first came into contact with Wren in connection with the chapel at Pembroke College, Cambridge. This structure, funded by a bequest from Bishop Matthew Wren, was built in two years, from 1663. It is often said to be Wren's first architectural commission, although his silence over the matter suggests that he may have played a relatively minor role. Pearce provided the decorative carving throughout and may have been responsible for much of the design.[11] As a statuary mason, Pearce kept a shop in Arundel Street, London, in which he employed four men and sold sculpture and funerary monuments. It is, however, portrait busts for which he is known – such as the portrait of Wren that now sits in the Ashmolean Museum in Oxford – rather than large, fashionable marble tombs. Although he would have been more than capable of executing the carving at St Paul's, he would probably have delegated the task to others, like all the other mason-contractors. He was also a competent architect in his own right, and Wren used him to make a number of drawings for the new cathedral.[12]

The last group of masons to work at St Paul's, which included Nathaniel Rawlins, Thomas Wise junior, Samuel Fulkes, Thomas Hill, Ephraim Beauchamp and John Tompson, all made their living – as far as we can tell – exclusively from building work. All of them seem to have bought their freedom in London by redemption rather an apprenticeship to London masons. Wise, Hill, Beauchamp and Tompson were members of the Masons' Company, while Fulkes and Rawlins belonged to the Haberdashers' Company. With the exception of Rawlins, who was a pupil of Jasper Latham, they all worked for Wren elsewhere.[13]

All the mason-contractors oversaw a number of jobs at any one time and many had considerable interests elsewhere, so that the individuals who appear in the records could not have devoted more than a small portion of their time to the cathedral. We know from the records that they employed foremen who paced the site inspecting work as it was carried out. Pearce, Marshall, Strong and others would have turned up periodically to check on progress, and presumably they met with the Surveyor on Saturdays, when he made his weekly trip to the cathedral.[14]

These, then, were the master masons, the heads of their building firms. We know their names and much about their lives because they kept records, but it is much more difficult to find information concerning the men they employed. In fact, we know less about them than we do about the labourers at St Paul's because payment by measure required that only the amount of work carried out should be recorded. Individual masons' names do not appear in the cathedral's general accounts, although they would no doubt have been set down in the account books kept by the master masons for their own benefit.

Occasionally we gain some insight into the numbers and types of masons employed from other sources. One such is the Search Records of the Masons' Company, which during the course of a census of all the masons working in the City on 26 September 1694 made a visit to St Paul's. There, they found that Edward Strong had 66 masons on site, Kempster and Beauchamp had 24, Tompson had 13, and Fulkes, Hill and Wise each had 16. What was striking is how few of these masons had served apprenticeships and taken their freedom. The records are confusing in places, but of Strong's masons it seems that 17 were still apprentices, 18 were 'foreigners' (that is, qualified masons but from outside London) and only 15 were members of the Masons' Company. Of the remainder, the status of some went unrecorded, while 7 were said to be freemen of the City of London but members of other Companies (3 were Haberdashers, 2 Clothworkers and 2 Leathersellers). It is clear that the traditional route of working as an apprentice, taking one's freedom and then joining the guild had been thrown into chaos by the Great Fire. Frustratingly, the one thing this list does not provide is any notion of the hierarchy that might have existed within the teams operating at St Paul's.[15]

Records from the medieval period split ordinary masons into layers, hewers and carvers. The layers mostly worked on unfinished rubble walls, whereas the hewers (later called 'banker masons'), who seem to have been more skilled, worked the stone on low benches. The hierarchy does not seem to have been so rigidly defined at St Paul's, however: only skilled carvers are named – men like Edwin Arnold, Caius Gabriel Cibber, Edward Bird and Jonathan Maine – although no doubt some of the work attributed to them was actually executed by their apprentices and assistants.[16]

Masons' work was carried out in wooden huts constructed for the purpose around the site, referred to in the accounts as 'sheds' rather than the traditional 'lodges'. Stone arrived from the quarry sawn roughly to size, which the masons would shape more accurately, either following straightforward measurements for simple rectangular blocks or using wooden templates for more complicated forms.[17]

The masons were expected to provide their own tools, which would be kept sharp by the site's blacksmith. They used steel-tipped chisels and wooden mallets that would still be familiar to masons working today. Chisels came in many sizes and shapes: small, narrow chisels to exert maximum pressure and to roughly shape the stone, and broader chisels to finish it. Basic shaping was often carried out using grub-saws – toothless

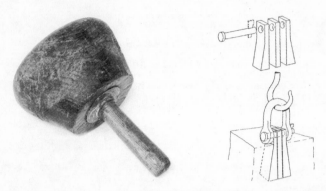

A typical seventeenth-century stonemason's maul (above left). This example is said to have been used by Wren to lay the foundation stone of St Paul's. Above right is a lewis, used for lifting stone since the Middle Ages.

saws that relied on sand and friction to cut slowly through the stone. Pieces of stone were moved around the site on elm rollers before being hoisted onto the scaffolds with 'lewises', just as they had been in the Middle Ages.[18]

Each team of masons had access to a tracing floor, which was enclosed in a kind of shed to protect it from the weather. The tracing floors at St Paul's were large, smooth wooden floors on which parts of the building could be mapped out full scale. Cut stones could then be aligned on the tracing floor to check that they were the right size before being winched aloft. Each stone would finally be set in place by masons balancing high up on swaying rickety scaffolds. As much work as possible was done on the ground, but the carving of continuous mouldings and ornaments – such as the fluting of columns – was always completed *in situ* to ensure that the sections lined up precisely. Wren seems to have required much of the carving to be done later, possibly to speed up the works and to allow some design decisions to be delayed as long as possible.[19] Balancing high up on a rickety scaffold, the masons who carved these intricate details relied entirely on the skill of another set of craftsmen: the carpenters. Their work is easily overlooked since it has mostly disappeared, taken down as the cathedral rose higher.

10

CARPENTERS AND SCAFFOLDING

In the seventeenth century, builder-woodworkers were divided into two categories – carpenters and joiners – and the two trades were often in dispute over where one group's responsibilities ended and the other's began. Joiners made furniture, panelling and door surrounds, generally operating in workshops and only bringing pieces on site to install them. Carpenters, on the other hand, always worked on site, where they had temporary workshops for storing timber and for working in bad weather; mostly, however, their work was in the open air on large-scale construction. They made up frames for roofs and floors and built the scaffolding.[1]

The building site of St Paul's was wholly reliant on timber – not so much for the few roofs and floors that still remain in place today, but primarily for temporary works: walkways through the mud that allowed the site to be cleared, fencing to keep out the young boys who were always falling into holes, and so on. As the building rose above ground level in the late 1670s, wood was used to construct the scaffolding and the great ramps that allowed materials to be carried up the outside of the building; it was also used for the temporary huts and houses that sheltered the workmen. Every brick or masonry arch or dome was made on a temporary timber formwork that would be dismantled on completion. Lastly, it was used to make the great cranes and hoists that enabled materials to be lifted to the upper reaches of the massive edifice. All this was the work of the carpenters.[2]

Sadly, the records for St Paul's are insufficiently detailed to enable an accurate reconstruction of the scaffolding or other temporary works. The accounts provide countless references to 'scaffolding', 'platforms', 'tressels', 'bridges', 'shedding', 'walkways', 'covering in the work' and 'centers'; only one picture survives, which is too small to be of much use. But the scaffolding at St Paul's probably differed little from the wooden scaffolding that was in use in Western Europe in the twentieth century and is still employed in some parts of the world today. It consisted of stout vertical timber poles ('standards') crossed with horizontal 'spars', lashed together into an H-shaped frame. The spars would extend beyond the scaffolding, either resting on an unfinished wall or passing through it to be fixed to standards on the other side. Planks were laid between the spars to provide a platform for standing on. Sources from the Middle Ages refer to basket-weave 'hurdles', which were used instead of planks, but nothing of the sort is mentioned in the St Paul's accounts. It must have been difficult to support pieces of stone weighing upwards of seven tons on such structures, so it seems likely that heavier blocks were lifted directly onto the stone walls.[3]

Men and bucketloads of materials were transported up and down the Great Stairs on the south side of the cathedral, which were accessed directly from Convocation House Yard via a door at ground level. These spiral stairs, which today are still the main way of ascending the dome, are wide enough for two heavily laden men to pass. At the top of the stairs the carpenters erected temporary 'bridges' at each level for the workers to cross to the various parts of the works. As the building rose vertically so the stairs were extended upwards, and the bridges were continually reconfigured to give access to the whole structure.[4]

Heavier materials that could not be carried were hoisted up using various types of lifting equipment. The accounts list 'sheeres', 'gibbets' and 'engines'. Shears were timber A-frames used in conjunction with a block and tackle to lift most normal loads; they were easy to move and could, if made large enough, lift very heavy stones. Gibbets could twist on pivot at the bottom, making it easier to offload the stone at the top of the building, but the pivot placed a limit on the maximum load that could be carried. The term 'engines' implied more complex systems of pulleys and gearing. These machines were capable of lifting the largest loads but were more difficult to move. Engines were put on the top of the south-west and north-east legs of the dome in February 1688. Again, there is too little information to be sure of the exact form these cranes took, but we do have contemporary pictures of French cranes of the type Wren would have seen used in the rebuilding of the Louvre, and it is not unreasonable to suppose that similar examples were employed at St Paul's. There are references to the use of capstans, but no mention is made of

View of the new cathedral from north-east, by Sutton Nicholls (1695) – the only surviving illustration of the scaffolding used at St Paul's. On the left is the choir, and on the right is the north transept. The perimeter fencing and builders' huts are clearly visible.

the giant wheels turned by manpower that drove the larger medieval cranes. Manpower was certainly used, however, since there were no horses on site at St Paul's – the only animals involved were carthorses that hauled materials to and from the works each day.[5]

Wren understood from the outset that the coordination of the scaffolding and cranes with the rest of the works was essential and he took two steps to ensure that everything ran smoothly. Firstly, he appointed a single Master Carpenter to head up all the carpentry operations on site. This was no place for competition. Secondly, he ordered that all carpenters should be paid by the day so that the Master Carpenter would never be tempted to allocate less labour than was required.

The man Wren selected for this important post was not at first sight the most obvious choice. John Longland had served an apprenticeship under Thomas Bates of the Haberdashers' Company, and had duly become a freeman of that Company in 1666. Nevertheless, as we have seen, membership of a livery company did not necessarily imply that he worked in that particular trade, and it is likely that Longland was a carpenter by training, not a haberdasher. Wren employed him on no fewer than fifteen of the City churches between 1670 and 1693, and by 1685 he had become one of the most prominent carpenters in England.[6]

Longland first appears in the accounts for the months of January, February and March 1672. His attendance was haphazard in the following years and amounted to no more than a few days each month. Relatively few carpenters were required on site at this stage, and no doubt he was engaged chiefly on supervising his other projects around the city. After 1675, when work on the cathedral began in earnest, it must quickly have become apparent that Longland could not oversee all his works without assistance, and so in January 1676 he was allowed to take on a partner, an experienced carpenter called Israel Knowles.[7]

Knowles was the son of Jacob Knowles, a haberdasher from Kingston, Surrey, and it may have been through that connection that he knew

Engraving of the construction of the east front of the Louvre in Paris. In the centre foreground is a capstan of the type known to have been used in St Paul's for hauling stone up to the top of the cathedral. To the right, masons are sawing through a large block of stone.

Longland. He had been apprenticed to one Benjamin Warden and was made a freeman of the Carpenters' Company in 1646. In time, he would duly join the Livery (1656) and serve as a warden (1677–78) and Master (1679). In the 1670s he was already undertaking contracts in his own right. He had worked on the Deanery of St Paul's in 1673 and took contracts at seven of Wren's City churches.[8]

Longland and Knowles acted in partnership only at St Paul's, running their businesses separately elsewhere. At the cathedral they were each paid 3s. a day and received 2s. 6d. for every man working under them. In the early days there were rarely more than twenty carpenters on site, but as work progressed and the walls rose higher so the amount of scaffolding that had to built, repaired and continually adapted increased.

The manual work was done by labourers, while the skilled craftsmen concentrated on cutting the timber to size and fitting it together. Longland and Knowles worked half a month each, presumably because the Surveyor required at least one of them to be on site at any one time. When Knowles died in 1692, Longland turned to another carpenter, Thomas Woodstock, to replace him. Woodstock had worked under Wren at St John Moore's School in Appleby, Leicestershire, and as an overseer on various other jobs. But the partnership was cut short when Woodstock died in 1694, leaving Longland once more without a partner. There being no obvious deputy at the time, Longland ran the contract alone until he selected Richard Jenings to work with him nine years later.[9]

Richard Jenings is one of the most fascinating figures involved in St Paul's. He was the son of Nicholas Jenings, a bargemaster in Henley-on-Thames in Oxfordshire. On 2 April 1695 Longland officially took him on from another carpenter, John Reading, as his own apprentice. Jenings first appears in the St Paul's accounts in March 1696, when he was fifth from the end of a list of thirty-five carpenters on site. By June 1702 he was head of a list of seventeen carpenters working on the dome, and just a year later Longland promoted him to be his full partner. Three years later, after thirty-one years of working on the cathedral, Longland died and Jenings was left in sole charge of the single most important carpentry contract in England at the time: the construction of the dome of St Paul's. His success, as we shall see, made him rich, but it also laid him open to accusations of corruption; and his involvement with St Paul's culminated in a scandal that led ultimately to his dismissal and to Wren leaving the works.[10]

Plate 1 Sir Christopher Wren;
portrait by Godfrey Kneller, 1711.
The architect's right arm is resting
on a plan of the west end of the
new St Paul's.

Plate 2 Portrait of Edward Strong
senior, one of the master masons at
St Paul's who made a considerable
fortune from building work after the
Great Fire.

Plate 3 The Great Model in its current home, the Trophy Room at St Paul's.

Plate 4 (opposite) Wren's pre-Fire design for the remodelling of St Paul's Cathedral, showing a new dome added to the existing fabric.

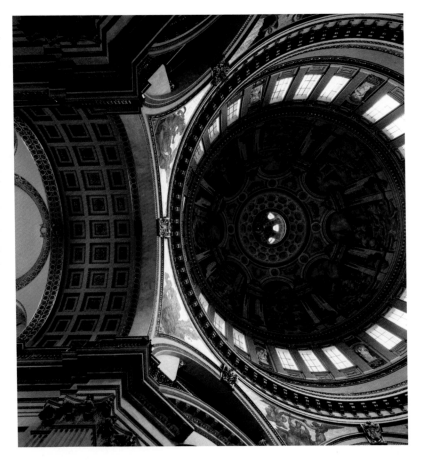

Plate 5 The inside of the dome, showing decorations painted by Sir James Thornhill between 1715 and 1721.

Plate 6 (opposite) The choir as it is today. The mosaics covering the spandrels and the ceiling were added at the end of the nineteenth century.

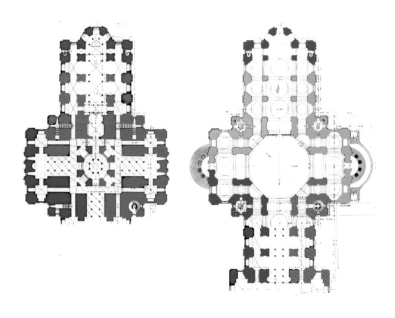

1675–78   1679–86

■ Thomas Strong

■ Joshua Marshall

■ Thomas Strong until 1681,
    thereafter Edward Strong

■ Edward Pearce

■ Jasper Latham

■ Thomas Wise sen.

Plate 7   Diagram indicating the division of work between the various mason-contractors who worked on St Paul's. While the plans are not intended to show the progress of construction, they do give a rough idea of the order in which the work was completed.

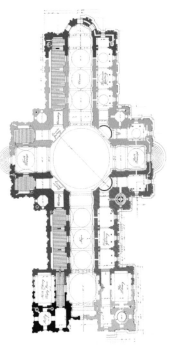

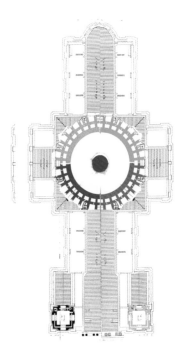

1687–99

1700–1716

- ■ Edward Strong sen.

- ▨ Edward Pearce until 1690, thereafter
  C. Kempster and E. Beauchamp

- ▨ Jasper Latham until 1690,
  thereafter Nathaniel Rawlins

- ■ Thomas Wise jun. and Thomas Hill

- ▨ John Tompson

- ■ Samuel Fulkes

- ■ Edward Pearce until 1690, thereafter
  Thomas Wise jun. and Thomas Hill

- ■ Edward Strong sen.

- ▨ C. Kempster and E. Beauchamp

- ▨ Nathaniel Rawlins

- ■ Thomas Wise jun. and Thomas Hill

- ▨ William Kempster

- ■ Samuel Fulkes

Plate 8 A view of the cathedral's west front and north-west tower, with the dome behind.

11

SOURCING THE MATERIALS

Just as money was an important factor in the time it took to build the cathedral, so equally was the supply of building materials. The task of ordering materials for the building of St Paul's fell to the Assistant Surveyor, who acted as the 'Purveyor' of the works. At the start of the rebuilding the Assistant Surveyor was Edward Woodroffe, but with his untimely death in 1676 the task passed to John Oliver, who managed it ably for twenty-five years. The position was a complicated one, which the Assistant Surveyor was expected to manage without 'travelling into the country'. Some materials were difficult to find and took years to get to site, while others, although more readily to hand, needed to be supplied continuously since any delay stopped work on site. There was also limited storage in the yards that had been walled off around the cathedral, and building materials often went missing. The Clerk of Works kept guard dogs, and eight nightwatchmen roamed the grounds to discourage thieves.

The most constant need on site was for a ready supply of timber, which was used for scaffolding, for shoring and temporarily propping up unfinished walls, and for building all the associated huts, fences, cranes, and so on. In the seventeenth century there was considerable concern surrounding the diminishing supply of timber and particularly the effect this might have on shipbuilding, which was, of course, critical for the nation's defences. The great forests were disappearing, the wood being used for construction, shipbuilding, manufacturing and as fuel. Wren's friend, the diarist John Evelyn, published a book on the subject, calling for immediate action to safeguard the timber supply.[1] Modern historians continue to argue over the seriousness of the shortage, or indeed whether there was really a shortage at all.[2]

Throughout its history England had proudly boasted the superiority of English oak both for shipbuilding and for mainstream construction. Chestnut and elm were also used but oak was preferred, and one need look no further than the large number of surviving medieval timber houses to see its merits. But by the mid-seventeenth century softwoods were replacing oak in construction and much of that wood was being imported from the Baltic. The trade had begun in the Middle Ages but had increased significantly. Softwood for St Paul's was imported from Norwegian ports, including Christiania (modern Oslo), Dram and Fredrikstad. Some of it probably came ready-sawn, since water-powered mechanical sawmills had been used for centuries on the Continent. But English sawyers had always resisted their introduction fiercely, and much timber was still cut in the traditional manner, with pit-saws. The senior sawyer stood on the tree-trunk that was to be cut, which was either lifted up on trestles or placed over a pit. The apprentice or junior sawyer crouched underneath, and between them they moved the great saw up and down, the sawdust falling on the unlucky person below. It was slow work and required great skill. There were several saw pits at St Paul's, so evidently a reasonable quantity of timber still arrived uncut.[3]

For royal works (or works for a large landowner) the trees used would be sourced from local forests, and the carpenter would go out himself to choose the trees to be felled. This was obviously not practical at St Paul's, which instead had to rely on the existing network of London timber merchants. The procurement of very large timbers was always problematic. Indeed, the length of timbers for the tie-beams of roofs often set an effective limit on the width of a building in this period. Oak timbers 20 feet (6 m) long were commonly available, but larger sizes had to be specially sourced and the difficulty increased in proportion to the required length. Wren had already determined that the roofs of St Paul's should span 42 feet (13 m), requiring timbers 46 feet (14 m) in length, which was at the uppermost limit of what was practically achievable using English timber. In less important buildings Wren was happy to substitute softwood for oak, but for St Paul's he was understandably wary of compromise. John Longland, the Master Carpenter, was dispatched to choose the trees personally. Fifty trees were donated by the Duke of Newcastle from his forests at Welbeck in Nottinghamshire, and more long timbers were supplied by John Etty of York. Having trained as a carpenter, Etty had become a prominent architect in York, but like many carpenters of the period he acted as a timber merchant on the side. Etty's timber came by sea, while the Duke of Newcastle's donation had a complicated journey by road (each tree being pulled in a cart by a team of cattle) and river. The small size of seventeenth-century carts and the poor state of the country roads (which were simply dirt tracks) made all carriage by road extremely expensive. As a result, the duke's kind gift ended up costing almost as much as Etty's commercial transaction and involved Longland in weeks of expensive travelling to organize the delivery.[4]

Owing to the problems involved in road transport, almost all of the building materials came to St Paul's by boat. They were landed directly at the three wharves on the section of the river nearest to the cathedral. From there, supplies were transferred to carts that trundled up the steep hill to the cathedral itself, where the more valuable items would be locked away in the yard beside the office of works. Only occasionally was it necessary to close the streets and drag much heavier items up the hill on rollers using pulleys, an inconvenience that was avoided where at all possible. Materials that came by sea could not be landed directly at St Paul's Wharf because London Bridge obstructed passage: instead, ships had to offload their wares east of the bridge, where they were transferred to lighters (smaller barges) for transport upriver. Not surprisingly, the wharf owners – who effectively controlled the passage of goods – charged considerable fees for the use of their cranes.

The main provider of such services to St Paul's was a man called John Slyford. Slyford operated a wharf and crane a fair way downstream from London Bridge, at Redriffe Stairs in Rotherhithe. It was here that ships unloaded the building materials to be transferred onto barges (larger items by crane). When the tide was right, the barges continued upstream to the cathedral's wharf or to another wharf owned by Slyford a hundred yards or so upstream, where Barnard's Castle had been. There he had another large crane capable of lifting stones from the barges into horse-drawn carts, which were then hauled up the hill to the cathedral.[5]

In using Slyford, the cathedral simplified its operations. It only had to deal with one operator rather than pay separately for 'wharfage', 'lighterage' and 'cartage'. The arrangement gave Slyford a considerable

Map showing the location of the various docks used by St Paul's in relation to the cathedral and London Bridge.

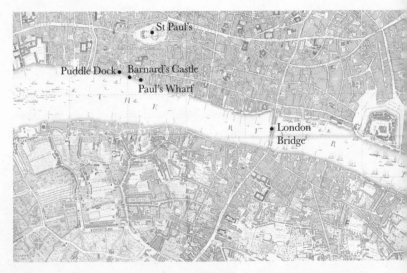

advantage in his relationship with the cathedral, but like the other workmen he had to put up with slow payment: by 1694 the cathedral owed him £700.[6]

In 1686 the Company of Carmen, London's transport livery, complained that Slyford was not a member and did not pay them any dues, thus infringing their monopoly, but the cathedral took no notice. A year later a competitor accused Slyford of embezzlement. Stone arrived at Slyford's wharves cut roughly to shape, but it was claimed that Slyford was in the habit of pretending that some of it had been broken in transit. It was said he would then sell on the perfectly good stone to other building sites around London. Slyford was investigated but nothing could be proved. Similar charges were made against him in 1693, but he was again cleared of all wrongdoing. These sort of accusations were completely normal for the time and there are many instances in the commissioners' minute books of claims being made against various members of the works.[7]

Wren's cathedral was built using stone from Burford and Headington in Oxfordshire; Reigate and Guildford in Surrey; Tadcaster in Yorkshire; the Isle of Portland in Dorset; Beer in Devon; Ketton in Rutland; near

Redriffe Stairs

Maidstone in Kent (Kentish rag); and Caen in France. Of these, only Portland, Ketton and Burford stone was employed on the exterior, the remainder being used for interior or infill works. It is a long-forgotten fact that St Paul's was originally two-toned, but the slightly darker Burford stone was affected by atmospheric pollution and started to crumble, and was entirely replaced by Robert Mylne, Surveyor from 1766 to 1811. Thus the cathedral we see today is not entirely as Wren designed it, although it is probably as he would have wished it to be had enough Portland stone been available.[8]

December 2° 1675 / A List of Scantling Block-Stones for ye Quire of St Pauls from the Plinth to the Architrave of the Isles

	Long	High	Deepe	Quantity in each Stone	Totall in Tunns	Moulds upon the Bed
Bases for 30 Pilasters	5.9	2.3	2.6 / 3.6	35°	73	
230 Stones for ye Bodies of 30 Pilasters	4.	4.	2.6 / 1.6	32	460	
230 Bend Stones for ye Same	4.	1.4	2.9 / 2.3	13.6	193	
66 Stones for ye Jambes of 11 Windows & ranging wth ye great Stones of ye pilasters	2.2	4.	2.6	27	112	
44 Ends Stones to bond the said Jambes of 11 Windows	2.2	1.4	3.	8.8	24	
22 higher End Stones under ye Way Carrs of ye Same	2.2	2.9	3.	18.	25	mould upon the Face
22 Impost Stones for ye Same	4.	4.6	2.6	35.	48	
22 Arch Stones for ye Same	5.6	3.	2.6	41.	56	
11 Key Stones for ye Same	3.	4.	4.	48	33	
30 Astragalls for ye Pilasters	5.	2.2	3.	32.	60	
30 Stones for ye under part of ye Capitalls	5.	1.6	3.6	26.	48	
30 Stones for ye upper parts of the Same	7.	3.6	3.6	86.	161	
			Totall of Tunns		1293	

A true Copy of the Originall delivered by Sr Chr: Wren, compared & examined this day above sd.
By John Tillison

A letter from Wren to his agent at Portland, dated 1675, setting out the sizes and shapes of stone required for the first section of the choir.

Two main types of stone are used in building works: sedimentary and volcanic. Sedimentary rocks are further subdivided into limestones and sandstones. Portland stone is an exceptionally fine limestone. Under the magnifying glass it can be seen to be composed of a large number of closely packed spheres, or oolites, and is thus sometimes called an oolitic limestone. What mattered to Wren and his masons were its texture, its workability, its general strength and its resistance to weathering. All these factors made Portland stone the perfect choice for the cathedral. But the deciding factor was that the quarries on the Isle of Portland belonged the Crown. Officially the stone was available to Wren for free, although – as with the timber offered by the Duke of Newcastle – 'free' turned out to be rather expensive. First, there were the costs of extraction – which included not only the labour needed to hew the stone from the rock, but also transportation in carts and the maintenance of wharves and cranes at Portland. Second, there were the costs of transporting the stone from Portland to London. Lastly, there was the expensive business, already described, of getting it from the ships to the cathedral.[9]

Quarrying the stone ought to have been to be simple. All that was needed was a labour force on the island working diligently at an agreed rate, which would ensure a steady supply of stone being dispatched to the cathedral. Stone on Portland was extracted in the traditional manner: holes were drilled down into the rock using augers (long, hand-turned drills), and then wedges were inserted to split off blocks from the cliff face.

But problems arose from the commissioners' insensitivity to the islanders' customs, which led to local hostility and resistance that continued throughout the works. The Isle of Portland is not an island proper, but rather a huge outcrop of limestone joined to the south coast by a causeway. Its near separation from the mainland allowed it to maintain a number of distinct customs that carried legal weight. One of these related to common land belonging to the Manor of Portland, on which every inhabitant had rights to graze and to dig stone. Furthermore, the

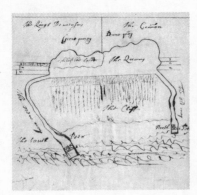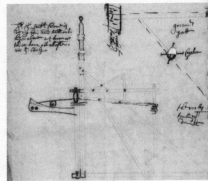

Left A map of the Isle of Portland drawn by an unknown hand and sent to Wren. Two piers are marked – a south pier on the left and a north pier on the right – implying that the quarry used was on the east side of the island, not the west, as is usually assumed. *Right* Thomas Gilbert's drawing, made in 1678, of the crane at Portland, sketched in elevation and, on the right, in plan. It shows a gibbet that pivoted on a mast, with pulleys attached to a capstan.

islanders were entitled to a portion of the duty paid to the Crown on stone removed from Portland. The duty was 12*d*. per ton, of which they received 9*d*. This money was paid into a fund administered by the Court Leet on the island and used to benefit the inhabitants. Stone for royal use was of course exempted from the duty.[10]

The commissioners' minute book records that the grant of stone to St Paul's was conferred on 24 February 1675, and the commissioners duly appointed one Thomas Knight, a well-known London mason and stone-merchant, to act as their agent on the island. The agreed rate for extracting the stone and shipping it to London was 10*s*. 2*d*. per ton for ordinary block and 11*s*. 6*d*. for stone that was 'scappled', or roughly cut to shape. Almost immediately problems arose. First, the pier at Portland proved wholly inadequate for the huge amount of stone to be transported, and money had to be provided for its rebuilding. More seriously, by 1677 it had already become clear that Knight was unreliable. Stone was ordered in letters that set out the exact sizes and shapes to be dispatched, but Knight was failing to keep proper accounts or to send the stone that was required. The commissioners also suspected him of fraud.[11]

A legal dispute arose, which became more and more complex. The islanders, convinced that their rights were being infringed, continually disrupted supply of stone and in 1678 even resorted to violence. Knight was replaced by one agent and then by another, without any resolution being achieved. To complicate matters further, a storm in 1696 wrecked the quays and cranes, and Wren was obliged to go down to Portland himself to sort things out. The islanders continued to be uncooperative

Map showing the sources of stone used in the rebuilding of St Paul's Cathedral.

and even threatening on occasion. However, by 1708 the need for stone at St Paul's was diminishing, and in 1714 the cathedral's right to stone from the quarries finally expired. Thus ended a legal relationship that had lasted for thirty-six years, most of which had been spent in dispute. No doubt all parties were relieved to see it end.[12]

When it came to the supply of stone, the men at Portland were only part of the problem: transport was also a major cause for concern. In the harbour in Portland the stone had to be loaded into small sailing ships called barks. The number of ships required by the works at St Paul's placed a considerable strain on local resources, so that vessels of varying sizes had to be used. Although the average ship was able to take about 36 tons of stone, the commissioners later had pay for some ships to be modified to take particularly large pieces and for repairs to vessels that had been damaged during loading and unloading.[13]

Once they had been loaded at Portland, the ships sailed along the south coast and up the Thames Estuary, travelling as far as Slyford's docks at Rotherhithe. Even allowing for a fair wind, this journey would take several days, and bad weather could add considerable delay. Ensuring a continuous supply of stone was thus extremely difficult. Occasionally ships were lost at sea, meaning that replacement stone had to be reordered and recut. A further and not inconsiderable danger was enemy action. On one notable occasion, a ship full of stone was captured by French privateers and taken to Calais. The captain, a certain Henry Perry, was exchanged for other prisoners and returned to England while his ship and cargo were sold to a Dutch merchant. The enterprising Captain Perry then went to Holland, bought back both ship and stone from the merchant, and sailed back to London, where he safely delivered the cargo to St Paul's and was duly paid. The ship, appropriately enough, was called 'the Phoenix of London'.[14]

12

COLLAPSING VAULTS AND
FLYING BUTTRESSES

In 1680, five years after construction had begun, the east end of St Paul's was beginning to take shape: the walls of the choir and the piers that would support the dome had reached the springing point of the arches, while the outer walls of the north and south transepts had been finished to the floor level of the cathedral.[1]

In January of the previous year, demolition work on the nave of the old cathedral had reached the Convocation House. Since the new cathedral lay at an angle to the foundations of the old, the walls of the south aisle of the new nave lay well within Convocation House Yard, where the office of works was sited. In fact, the line of the new building abutted the Convocation House itself, where the Great Model was on display. Two of eight stone buttresses supported the upper floor of the chapter house and prevented the crypt and foundations from being dug, so Wren decided to replace them with wooden props. A third buttress was demolished in April 1682, leaving the remaining parts of the old chapter house teetering on the edge of the excavated site, held back from toppling into the hole only by slender timber legs. It would remain propped up this way for the next eight years. Finally, a new timber building was constructed and the Great Model was slid into it on runners across a bridge, allowing the old

Convocation House to be demolished. A timber fence now formed one side of the much-reduced Convocation House Yard to stop people falling down the hole where the crypt was being constructed.[2]

The crypt of the new cathedral consisted of stone walls filled with rubble, like the rest of the construction, but the vault was made of brick. The chief reason for this was almost certainly one of economy. Stone vaults would have been more time-consuming and therefore more costly to construct. Stone was always laid with narrow joints, and making such a vault involved tapering each stone to fit with its neighbour. While this was perfectly possible – one only has to look at the Gothic cathedrals to see outstanding examples of stone vaulting – it was far easier and cheaper to use bricks. In a brick vault, the curvature can be created by tapering the joints rather than the bricks themselves, doing away with the necessity of cutting altogether. All that was required was a ready supply of good bricks, strong, reliable mortar and a team of skilled bricklayers.[3]

Work had begun on the crypt vaults in 1676, and much of the crypt under the dome was built in 1678. Between 1676 and January 1679, over 984,000 bricks were delivered on site for construction of these vaults, the upper part of which formed the floor of the cathedral. The bricks supplied were of two types: 'stock' bricks and 'place' bricks. It is not exactly clear what the terms meant and historians disagree over their definitions, but what is clear is that place bricks were inferior, in 1675 costing 13*s.* per thousand, 6*s.* less than stock bricks.[4]

In the seventeenth century all bricks were made by hand. Brick earth was dug in the autumn and left over winter in the frost. It was then trodden under foot to break it up, small stones being removed at the same time. In London it was not uncommon for the brickmaker to mix in some ash (termed 'rubbish') at this point, which would contain unburnt coal. This saved fuel and helped the brick to be fired more evenly. Next, the bricks were moulded in open-frame moulds. Place bricks may have been moulded directly onto the ground, while stock bricks were probably moulded on a table that supported a timber block called a 'stock'. The moulds were then turned out onto small wooden boards called pallets and the bricks on their pallets placed on barrows to be taken out to dry on the ground. The period of drying varied from a few days to a few weeks according to the weather, after which the new bricks were fired.[5]

Bricks might be fired in permanent kilns, but more commonly a temporary kiln called a 'clamp' was made out of wet bricks stacked up in such a way that the fuel could be burned within. The advantage of clamp building was that it was cheap and did not require a permanent structure, but one disadvantage was that bricks on the outside were under-fired while those next to the flames tended to be reduced to glass. To avoid such problems, larger projects often constructed their own kilns where land was available. This was not the case at St Paul's, which instead relied on a steady supply from the massive brick industry that had grown up to rebuild the City after the Great Fire.[6]

Place bricks were delivered directly to St Paul's by cart, with transport included in the price, but the stock bricks, which were often made in Kent, arrived by river at Puddle Dock, between St Paul's Wharf and Barnard's Castle. Kentish stock bricks were provided by Messrs Woodforde and Rawlins, while the suppliers of the place bricks were not recorded.[7]

The bricklaying was under the control of the Master Bricklayer, a position occupied by three men during the works (see table overleaf). The first, Thomas Warren, also worked for Wren on St James Garlick Hill, St Michael Queenhythe and St Peter Cornhill. He seems to have died sometime in 1683: payments after this date are signed for by his widow, but he may have been ill for sometime, because he last appears in the accounts himself in January 1682. The little brickwork there was to do in the period 1683–86 was given to small contractors, so it was not until 1686 that a new Master Bricklayer was appointed: John Bridges, who took over to supervise the choir vaulting. He had worked for Wren at St Michael Queenhythe, St Mary Abchurch and St Michael Bassishaw.

Period	Master Bricklayer	Main responsibility
1675–83	Thomas Warren	Vaulting of crypt under choir, transepts and dome
1686–88	John Bridges	Upper vaulting over choir and aisles
1688–91	Richard Billinghurst	Completing upper vaulting over choir and aisles
1691–95	Richard Billinghurst	Vaulting of crypt under nave and aisles
1696–99	Richard Billinghurst	Vaulting of great arches around dome
1700–1705	Richard Billinghurst	Upper vaulting of nave and aisles
1705–8	Richard Billinghurst	Construction of dome

Table showing the Master Bricklayers employed at St Paul's.

Unfortunately, he too died, in 1688, whereupon Richard Billingshurst assumed the role, remaining the cathedral's Master Bricklayer until 1721. Billinghurst also collaborated with Wren at Greenwich Hospital.[8]

The vaulting of the crypt was difficult, and in 1679 part of it collapsed, an event vividly described in Roger North's biography of his brother:

> [Sir Dudley North] was so great a Lover of building that St Paul's, then well advanced, was his ordinary walk. There was scarce a course of stones laid, while we lived together, over which we did not walk. And he would always climb to the uttermost heights ...
>
> We usually went there on Saturdays, which were Sir Christopher Wren's Days, who was the Surveyor; and we

commonly got a snatch of discourse with [Sir Christopher Wren], who like a true philosopher, was always obliging and communicative, and, in every matter we inquired about, gave short, but satisfactory, answers ... [North] observed that the great arches at the floor of St Paul's ... after the centres were struck, fell in twice; and he was much puzzled to find out the reason of it; which he did, and then fancied the builders themselves [still] did not [understand] it, till after the second fall had showed it them. It seems such things were not to be talked of there, and no subject of discourse with the workmen.[9]

It has been suggested that the collapse of the vaults was caused by water penetrating the mortar. If vaults are well constructed, however, the mortar is not of great importance. It seems more likely that the centering on which the vaults were constructed was removed before the spaces above the vault had been properly backfilled, leading the thin shells of the vaults to distort and fail. The part played by the backfill may not have been understood at the time. In any event, the accounts show that the vaults had to be rebuilt.[10]

The protracted length of time that St Paul's took to build was caused by problems with finance, but there is little doubt that the slower pace of construction also brought many advantages. First, the builders had time to rectify mistakes – such as the faulty vaulting – as they went along. Second, there was time to reassess the whole design continually as work progressed. Until recently, Wren scholars had argued that, by the time work began on site in 1675, the cathedral had been designed much as we see it today, and that subsequent alterations were confined mostly to the dome and west towers. That is how the project would have progressed under a modern building contract, but it misunderstands the way contracting worked at St Paul's.[11]

A comparison of the old cathedral (left) with the new (right), drawn by Godfrey Allen, showing the flying buttresses and screen walls (*The Builder*, 18 January 1924).

It is now apparent that Wren exploited every opportunity throughout the works to modify and improve his design, and that some of his most significant changes belong to the mid- to late 1680s – a decade after work began. The two alterations that had biggest impact on the outside appearance of the finished building were the addition of the libraries at the west end and the creation of the screen walls. Both seem to be associated with the new impetus given to the work by the accession of James II.[12]

The cathedral that was under construction until 1685 appears to have been a modified version of the Warrant design. The west end terminated in a pair of towers and a portico, and the roofs of the aisles were exposed, along with the prominent attached buttresses that supported the upper walls of the nave and the choir on each side. The first major change Wren introduced was the insertion of flying buttresses.

Flying buttresses were first employed in the Middle Ages and were a prominent feature of many Gothic cathedrals. The weight of the vaults and the wind loads acting on the walls of the nave clerestory were carried in arched buttresses over the aisles (hence 'flying') to the outside walls, where they could be transmitted to ground level without interrupting internal circulation. Old St Paul's had flying buttresses in the choir and at the crossing, where they had been inserted to help hold up the tower, but not in the Romanesque nave. Flying buttresses were incompatible with the Classical style in architecture, and so when Inigo Jones classicized the old cathedral he seems to have limited his interventions to adding ornaments to the Romanesque nave with its round-arched windows and attached buttresses. Sometime between the Warrant design and the mid-1680s, Wren seems to have decided that the new cathedral needed flying buttresses to reinforce the upper parts of the cathedral, but this left him with a similar problem.

James II was an enthusiastic supporter of the new cathedral, and it was almost certainly through his intervention that two chapels were added to the west end flanking the nave. (It has even been suggested that James may have intended one of them to be Roman Catholic.) Above these chapels Wren was to provide two libraries, one probably for the dean and one for the cathedral. (In the end, only one was fitted out as a library, the other becoming the new home for the Great Model.) The earliest drawings for the libraries appear in this period. It may have been the addition of these two-storey structures that led Wren to continue the line of the upper library cornice around the building, thus creating the so-called 'screen walls'. These give the cathedral an external appearance of uniform volume, whereas in fact the space behind is not roofed but open to the sky. They also served another purpose: to hide the flying buttresses. Evidence for the design changes made at this late stage rests on analysis of a set of drawings originally ascribed to Wren, but which are now thought to be by his greatest pupil and draughtsman, Nicholas Hawksmoor, who did not move into the office until many years later.[13]

Nicholas Hawksmoor (1662?–1736) was thirty years younger than Wren, and his background was far less promising. He was born in East Drayton in Nottinghamshire, the son of a smallholder. Little is known about his early life; from the fact that he could read Latin, French and a smattering of Italian, and that he had a reasonably good grounding in applied mathematics, it is assumed that he went to the local grammar school. His first employment was as a junior clerk to Samuel Mellish, a Doncaster Justice, and it was there that Hawksmoor seems to have met Edward Gouge, a celebrated decorative plasterer, who brought him to London and may also have introduced him to Wren. He first appears as Wren's personal assistant in 1684, when he moved into servant's lodgings either within, or attached to, his master's premises in Whitehall. Here, Hawksmoor quickly acquired the necessary draughting skills and became Wren's most valuable assistant. Wren in return gave him the finest education any aspiring young English architect could hope for, including access to Wren's extensive library and print collection and the opportunity of working in every capacity on the largest and most prestigious buildings of the day. In every respect Hawksmoor rose to the challenge.[14]

The screen walls with their concealed flying buttresses, which first appeared in Hawksmoor's drawings and became a crucial part of the

The space behind the screen walls, showing buttresses supporting the vault of the choir.

cathedral as built, have not been to everyone's taste. They were viciously attacked in the nineteenth century in the writings of A. W. N. Pugin, who accused Wren of structural dishonesty in the way 'one half of the edifice is built to conceal the other'. Pugin hated classicism and wanted a return to the Gothic style, claiming in his persuasive rhetoric that it was the only true Christian architecture. Oddly, Pugin's ideas concerning honesty in

Gothic buildings and the need for architecture to display its structure later became important features of modernism, and thus modernist critics still find Wren's screen walls difficult to understand. But such ideas would have been entirely alien to Wren. For him, Classical architecture was the only true architecture, and buildings did not exhibit their structure any more than mammals exhibited their skeletons externally. It was the consistency of the architecture that mattered, and the power of the visual effects it created. The means by which these effects were achieved was a matter not of honesty but of ingenuity, and the screen walls were an ingenious solution to a difficult problem.[15]

Wren's screen walls may also had a financial advantage. Just as they hid the flying buttresses, they also hid the upper parts of the nave and choir. Since these were no longer in view, they no longer needed to be decorated: they were thus easier to construct and could be completed more quickly. The ornate screen walls would be added later, as and when they could be afforded. Far from being an irrational fix for one inconvenient problem, they were actually a highly efficient solution to several apparently intractable ones.[16]

By 1690 all parts of the cathedral had risen above ground level. At the west end the walls of the Consistory Court and Morning Prayer Chapel were well under construction, while at the east end the external walls were much further advanced. It finally began to seem like it might be possible to complete the choir.

13

THE RACE TO FINISH
THE CHOIR

The rejection of the Great Model design and the new plans that followed it were based on the idea that St Paul's should be built from east to west, so that the choir could be opened for services as soon as possible. Yet in 1690, twenty-four years after the old cathedral had burnt down and fifteen years after rebuilding had begun, the choir was still very far from finished. Indeed, the whole works were affected by a twofold crisis, as we have seen: the political upheaval surrounding the accession of William III, which had caused Sancroft to resign as archbishop of Canterbury; and the ongoing urgency of renewing the Coal Tax so that further loans could be secured. It was clear that the choir had to be finished if the commissioners wanted to persuade Parliament to finance the works' completion.[1]

The masonry walls of the choir were completed by 1690 but the main space still had to be covered. The vault over the middle of the choir consists of four stone arches, between which are three shallow saucer domes of brick. A series of smaller saucer domes form the ceilings in the side aisles. Both the stone arches and the vaults were constructed before the roof was put on: this left them temporarily open to the weather, but made the building of the roof safer. It gave the carpenters substantial to stand on, rather than working at height precariously perched on scaffolding.[2]

The aisles were completed first. The brick vaults on the north side of the choir were finished in September 1686. The centers for the brick vaults over the main part of the choir were erected in January and February 1692, and the timber roof above was completed in October. By July 1694 work was sufficiently complete for the great platform under the vaults that the plasterers had stood on to be demolished. At the same time carpenters began to build the huge timber partition wall that would separate off the choir from the rest of the building site.[3]

The joinery work could not begin until this partition was in place and the choir was weather-tight. By December 1694 the choir was sufficiently enclosed for carpenters to begin constructing the stalls. It was still rather draughty, however, since glass had not yet been fitted in the windows.[4]

Not all windows in the seventeenth century were glazed, but by Wren's time glass was well within the grasp of the middle classes.[5] There were three different types in production: cylinder glass, crown glass and plate glass. Cylinder glass could never be made completely flat, but its slight curve made it particularly useful for bow windows. The very best glass was plate glass, which was cast, but its cost and weight precluded its use in the huge windows of St Paul's. Instead, Wren elected to use crown glass, which was cheaper than plate glass but better than cylinder glass.[6]

Crown glass – like cylinder glass – is made by a glassblower, but instead of blowing a cylinder, he spins a blob of molten glass swiftly round on a spindle so that it spreads out into a flattened disc. When cooled, the resulting circular sheet can be cut into rectangles, Crown glass can be recognized by the circular patterns produced by the spinning. It was usually transported to site as uncut discs, which could be up to 6 feet (1.8 m) in diameter, packed in straw in flat wooden crates. Twenty-two cases of crown glass were bought from the 'Honoble [*sic*] Craven Howard Esq. and Company' and delivered to site in October 1694.[7]

The ironwork window frames were made by the Jean Tijou, the master craftsman who supplied much of the cathedral's wrought-iron decoration. They were set in position with spigots inserted into holes drilled into the stonework and fixed with molten lead. Some of the windows are over 22 feet (6.7 m) high and 12 feet (3.7 m) wide, with the ironwork alone weighing some 18 cwt (914 kg). The main window structure consisted of a pair of iron trusses forming the mullions, connected together at the top by an arched truss and two short transoms of a similar design that fixed to the stone surround. Each frame was finished with several coats of oil paint to prevent it from rusting. All these sections were cleverly designed so that they could be taken apart for ease of carriage (they were made in Hampton Court and brought down river by boat) and installation. The ironwork for each window alone cost £67, a very considerable amount of money, and the first was not installed in the choir until August 1691.[8]

Once the frames were in place, the glass could be fitted – a process overseen by Matthew Jarman, the chief glazier. He or his men would have carefully unpacked each case of glass and, using a diamond-tipped pen, scored and broke the discs into rectangular pieces in such a way as to minimize waste. Each of Wren's windows was divided into 5 × 8 inch (13 × 20 cm) rectangular quarries. Most of the work was carried out in November and December 1694, when Jarman installed 3,799 square feet (353 m²) of crown glass in twenty windows in the choir, using 322 square feet (30 m²) of waste pieces to glaze the upper windows lighting the roof space. He also installed 346 square feet (32 m²) of Newcastle glass in huge windows in the timber partition that separated the choir from the dome. In line with the practice of the time, the great windows of St Paul's all consisted of clear glass to let in the maximum amount of light, although some would be replaced by more elaborate stained glass in the Victorian era.[9]

Once the windows had been installed, the internal timberwork could begin. In April 1695 the carpenters began making the basic structure framing the screen and stalls, whereafter the decorative timberwork –

the joinery – could begin. In the seventeenth century joiners were involved in the making of panelling and other decorative elements that were glued and pinned together, as distinct from the rough structural work done by carpenters. Before 1695 there had rarely been more than a couple of joiners at St Paul's at any one time, and they had been employed mostly in making templates for the masons (in 1696 the resident joiners were Charles Hopson and Nathaniel Hemming). The construction of the choir stalls, however, obviously required a larger number of craftsmen.[10]

Work began in late summer 1696. In August, Roger Davis, Hugh Webb and Charles Hopson all received payment for making models of parts of the woodwork in the choir stalls and the pulpit; and Grinling Gibbons, the legendary carver, set about drawing the decoration that would complete them.[11]

Grinling Gibbons (1648–1721) was born in Rotterdam and moved to England sometime around 1669. He was discovered by chance in 1671 by Wren's friend John Evelyn, who saw him through the window of a rundown cottage in Deptford carving a timber version of Tinteretto's *Crucifixion* by candlelight. Evelyn described how he was so struck by the brilliance of the work that he went in and asked how much Gibbons would take for it. (Gibbons wanted £100, an enormous sum at the time.) Evelyn introduced the carver to the king and made Wren promise to employ him. His extraordinary ability (Gibbons's favourite trick was carving lace ruffs out of wood so convincingly that they were mistaken for the real thing) quickly made him the most sought-after carver in England. Moreover, he was skilled in working in stone as well as wood and at St Paul's would carve both.[12]

The timberwork for the stalls was divided into sections, with different contractors working to agreed patterns. In total, the woodwork of the choir cost £8,629 11s. $^1/_2$d. It is Gibbons who is normally credited by tour guides with the major part of the work, whereas in fact only £2,992 11s.

The choir at a thanksgiving service attended by Queen Anne in 1708, from an engraving by Robert Trevitt published in 1710. The many levels of seating are clearly visible, as is the great organ screen on the right.

$4^1/_2 d.$ was paid to him. It is clear that much of the carving was done by the others – Hopson, Davis and Webb, for example – who have been largely forgotten.[13]

The choir stalls were constructed in oak with carved decoration in limewood. They were in every respect most remarkable structures: two rows of pews with boxes and galleries above, and an ingenious system of sliding retractable seats that could be pulled out from underneath the stalls onto the floor of the choir when required. Gibbons's limewood carvings stand out, although his great innovation is not often appreciated: that of making the carvings in many separate layers, each held to its neighbour by little metal pins. The apparently deep undercutting is thus achieved by building up layers rather than by carving from a single piece of timber. The relatively soft nature of the limewood enabled him to create the particularly delicate flowers and garlands for which he is so justly famous.[14]

For one significant feature of the choir – the altar – Wren's original intentions are obscure. *Parentalia* mentions that he originally prepared a magnificent design 'consisting of four pillars wreathed in the richest Greek marbles, supporting a Canopy hemispherical', for which drawings and models were produced, but that the whole design was abandoned because the marble could not be obtained.[15] An incomplete wooden model survives.[16] A baldacchino was finally constructed in the late nineteenth century. The structure currently dominating the east end is a twentieth-century replacement following bomb damage during the Second World War. We do not know exactly what Wren intended, so both additions were based on imaginative interpretations.

Another sad loss is the organ case, which was taken apart in the 1860s to open up the choir. Constructed to Wren's designs, it was the choir's most dramatic element. It housed a much-praised instrument by Bernard Smith, an elderly organbuilder who proved rather slow. Despite having been contracted in 1694 and paid a substantial sum of money, Smith had still not finished the organ satisfactorily in 1698.[17]

The first service to be held in the cathedral – to celebrate the Peace of Ryswick – took place on 2 December 1697. John Evelyn mentions in his diary that Sunday services resumed three days later, on 5 December 1697. The organ, although only partially complete, was playable, even if the choir was still awkwardly divided from the dome by the temporary wooden screen that would remain in place until 1705. St Paul's may now have been open for business, but in 1700 it was still very far from complete. The design of the dome had not been finalized, and much of the cathedral had yet to be roofed.[18]

14

PROBLEMS ROOFING
THE CATHEDRAL

A typical timber roof in a late seventeenth-century house consisted of a series of triangular frames with a horizontal member, called a 'collar', connecting the two principal rafters about halfway up. These frames – or 'trusses', as they are often termed – are linked together along the length of the roof, at the level of the eaves, by the wall-plate resting on top of the walls, and higher up by one or more horizontal members, called 'purlins', that are usually mortised into the side of the trusses. The purlins carry common rafters, which in turn support the roof covering (consisting either of laths on which the tiles or slates are laid, or of boarding to support lead). This simple structural arrangement is known as a collar-braced roof and is perfectly adequate for spans up to about 20 feet (6 m), the maximum likely to be found in domestic architecture. Larger spans – such as those at St Paul's – required more complicated structures.[1]

At the beginning of the seventeenth century, before Italian-inspired Classical architecture had become the fashion in England, carpenters were still using arch-braced and hammer-beam roofs for long-span structures. These had altered little since the great roof of Westminster Hall – the largest spanning roof in Europe in the Middle Ages – which

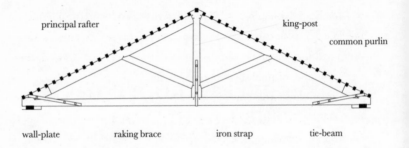

A king-post truss used in the choir of St Paul's.

had been constructed between 1397 and 1399. A superb example of a late hammer-beam roof can be found in the dining hall of Trinity College, Cambridge, constructed in 1615. In steeply pitched hammer-beam roofs, the structure is openly displayed and indeed celebrated.[2]

The new Italianate architecture that Inigo Jones popularized in England called for low-pitched roofs concealed behind parapets. Internally, the roof structure was no longer exposed but covered by heavy plaster ceilings that were often painted or elaborately decorated. All this called for a completely different type of roof structure: one that was still capable of spanning comparatively large spaces (30–40 feet, or about 9–12 m) like the hammer-beam roof, but which could do so within a modest height while supporting the considerable weight of the ceiling beneath. Recent research has shown that English carpenters of the period were unfamiliar with such structures and thus initially relied on the architects of the new buildings to provide detailed drawings from which they could work. In the seventeenth century it became established practice for the architect and not the carpenter to take responsibility for the structural adequacy of these designs, and thus architects had to familiarize themselves with the rudiments of structural carpentry.[3]

The most common structure adopted for this new type of roof was the king-post truss, which, like the new architectural style itself, came from Italy. There is no evidence of Italian carpenters being employed to work on English buildings – this would have been difficult considering the religious and political differences then dividing the two countries – so it is presumed that the main sources for designs were books. Indeed, there were a number of published sources available.[4]

The king-post truss consists of a central post (the king-post) that hangs from the top of the principal rafters. If all the members are properly constructed, the king-post should be in tension and thus help pull up the middle of the tie-beam, which otherwise would bow under the weight of the ceiling beneath. Raking braces attached to the bottom of the king-post also help reduce bending in the principal rafters. Traditionally, the carpentry was held in place entirely with timber pegs, but timber joints constructed in this way are weak in tension. Since the king-post truss relied on the joints being in tension, the whole structure required the use of iron straps.[5]

Inigo Jones seems to have been the first architect to use the king-post truss in England, for the Banqueting House in Whitehall (for which

An unusual view of the roof space above the choir, showing the upper part of the brick saucer domes and the king-post roof trusses. The plugs sticking out of the floor fill holes through which ropes were passed to suspend platforms for painting and to hoist materials up to the underside of the vaults.

structural drawings survive) and at the Queen's House in Greenwich. His trusses differ in a number of minor details from surviving Italian examples (chiefly in the way the top and bottom of the king-posts are formed), but work well. By Wren's time, the use of the king-post truss in the Office of Works was well established.[6]

At St Paul's, the nave, choir and transepts all have a clear span of 42 feet (13 m). This was a comparatively long span for a king-post truss, but well within its structural capabilities. The main problem was finding timbers large enough for the tie-beams, the longest members. The cross-sectional dimensions of a structural timber were called its 'scantling', and the required scantling of the tie-beams for St Paul's was some 12 × 12 inches (30.5 × 30.5 cm). Beyond 20 feet in length such beams were difficult to find. Each of them had to measure 46 feet (14 m) – 42 feet (13 m) of clear span plus 2 feet (0.6 m) of bearing at each end – and sourcing forty-eight of them for the main roof trusses presented a considerable challenge. Wren could easily have chosen to use two 23-foot (7 m) beams joined at the centre, and indeed this is a solution he used elsewhere – most notably at the Wren Library, Trinity College, Cambridge, which has a

The scissor-braced truss used to bridge the enlarged saucer dome at the west end of the nave.

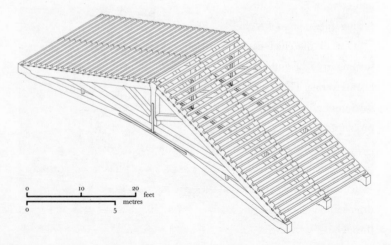

0   10   20 feet

0   5 metres

span similar to St Paul's. His reluctance to do so here was no doubt connected with his wish to ensure the longevity of the structure.[7]

The roof trusses of St Paul's are placed at intervals of 8 feet 6 inches (2.6 m) along the length of the cathedral. Rather than follow the normal arrangement of purlins and common rafters, Wren joined them together using a large number of horizontal common purlins – a system again derived from Italian examples.[8]

The cathedral's stone walls project above the vaults so that the tie-beams sit well above the top of the saucer domes in each bay. This sort of arrangement, in which a completely separate timber roof covers a stone vault beneath, is found in English medieval cathedrals, all of which have dramatic timber roof structures in huge spaces above the vaults. It was not the only way to do it: at St Peter's in Rome the timber roof rests on the vault itself, which then has to be thicker to support the weight. Wren's solution enabled him to keep the thickness of the vaults to a minimum.[9]

When Wren added the two libraries to the west end of the cathedral, he created a large saucer dome between them, forming an enlarged first bay for the nave. This large dome created a problem in the roof since its crown was higher than the tie-beams of the trusses, but Wren and his carpenter were able to devise an ingenious lifted tie-beam truss to avoid raising the whole roof at this point (see opposite).

One of the chief causes of the failure of king-post roofs is water seeping in at the gutters, which over time can lead to the ends of the tie-beams rotting. This is particularly a problem where the edge of the roof is surrounded by a parapet, as it is at St Paul's. Wren skilfully solved this problem by constructing a passage around the whole perimeter of the roof. Above this is a timber roof, easily inspected from beneath, built well below the ends of the trusses so that even if the gutters did leak, no major structural elements would be damaged. The stone floor of the passage drains into gullies, ensuring that any water that does get in is discharged through the walls to the outside of the cathedral.

Erecting the roofs at such a height would normally have presented a considerable challenge for the carpenters, but at St Paul's the vaults had been constructed first and provided a firm floor for them to stand on. Before work began, a model of the structure had been made for Wren's approval (supplied in a little box to protect it from damage). Then, following normal practice, the whole roof was made in parts at ground level. Each element was numbered and then disassembled. It was not uncommon for structures to be made up some distance away from site, but there was enough room at St Paul's for it to be done there. The parts were then hoisted up to the roof level and fitted together by carpenters using timber pegs. The iron straps were attached before the underside of the roof was boarded and ready for covering with lead.[10]

The first roofs were raised by carpenters working on day rates, but once the form had been established Wren found it more expedient to employ his master carpenters to complete the roofs of the nave and libraries 'by great', that is, for a lump sum. Progress on the roofs was determined largely by the masonry beneath (see illustration opposite), and once the timberwork of each was finished, the covering work could begin.[11]

From the outset Wren had intended to cover all the roofs in cast lead – a traditional material for cathedral roofs that was known to be long-lasting. It was made by pouring molten lead onto a sand-covered wooden casting table 12 to 15 feet (3.7 to 4.6 m) in length, surrounded by a wooden lip to contain the sand and lead. The sand was slightly damp, its exact humidity being important for a successful outcome. Milled lead, made using rollers that squeezed slabs of lead 5 inches (13 cm) thick into thin sheets, was newly available in England. Wren used it in Greenwich but was widely criticized for doing so, since milled lead was generally seen as an inferior, less durable alternative.[12]

Wren's decision to use cast lead at St Paul's encountered opposition from an unexpected quarter. In 1708, as the roof of the dome neared completion, the British copper industry successfully lobbied Parliament, and a

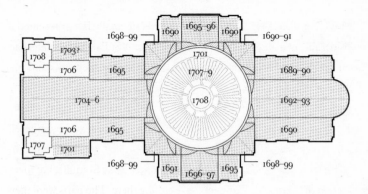

Plan showing the completion dates for the framing of the roofs.

House of Commons committee ruled that the great dome of St Paul's should be clad in their new product. On this point, however, the cathedral commissioners stood firm and supported their architect. A compromise was reached: lead would be used for the dome, but copper would be used for the crosses and finials on the western towers and the lantern.[13]

The thickness of lead was measured by weight in lbs per square foot. The contracts for the plumbers' work issued to Matthew and Joseph Roberts stipulated that all the lead for roofs was to be cast and had to weigh 11 lbs per square foot for the slopes and 9 lbs per square foot for the gutters. The dome was to be covered by Joseph Roberts in only the very best Derbyshire lead, which had to weigh 12 lbs per square foot.[14]

In designing the roofs Wren had carefully followed existing precedents while adapting them to the circumstances at hand. These simple structures have withstood the test of time remarkably well. But for one aspect of the design simple solutions were not available: the dome appears to have given him more cause for concern than any other part of the cathedral.

15

DESIGNING THE DOME

In March 1697 Parliament had voted to extend the Coal Tax at a much-reduced rate from 1700 to 1716 and to withhold half of the Surveyor's salary until completion of the works. At the next commissioners' meeting a despondent Wren reported that there would therefore be too little money to finish the cathedral before the extended Coal Tax expired. His estimated cost of the remaining works was some £171,255, while the income expected from the adjustments to the Coal Tax would amount to a total of only £144,224. Wren also reported that the workmen were now being paid so long in arrears that if nothing was done they might refuse to work altogether. By this date the structure below the dome had not risen much above the level of the arches over the nave and transepts. Wren told the commissioners that there was a choice to be made: either to finish the west end and the nave but leave the dome until later, or to stop work on the west end and finish the dome in the hope that the grandeur of the project's crowning glory would encourage public support for the completion of the cathedral as a whole.[1]

Wren rejected the idea of proceeding slowly with the whole work because of the enormous cost of scaffolding, particularly for the dome. In the wet English weather scaffolding lasted only a few years before the timbers rotted and became unsafe, whereupon the whole structure had to be rebuilt. As Wren pointed out, this would be a particular problem on the dome, which had to be constructed over a massive timber formwork at a great height, the failure of any part of which would be catastrophic.[2]

Wren had always seen the dome as the most important part of his great conception, and not surprisingly recommended that they complete the dome first and do so as quickly as possible. His arguments must have been persuasive because the commissioners agreed. Attention was now turned to the dome, and little was done on the west end during the next few years.

From the beginning, the great dome was to have been the crowning achievement of Wren's cathedral. It was to be the largest dome in England, the only other examples having been built by Wren himself. Of course, domes had a long and grand history. The Pantheon in Rome was then the largest dome in the world, with a diameter of 142 feet (43.3 m). Built by the emperor Hadrian between *c.* 118 and 125 AD, it possessed the most important interior surviving from antiquity and was frequently illustrated in prints and engravings, through which Wren and his contemporaries came to know Roman and Italian architecture. Perhaps the next greatest dome in history was that of Hagia Sophia in Istanbul, which Wren described in his historical tract on architecture. Built by the emperor Justinian in 532–537 AD, it spanned only 102 feet (31 m), but with its appended half-domes on either side it covered a dramatic space far larger than the Pantheon.[3]

Both these ancient structures had inspired the Renaissance and its first great architect, Brunelleschi, whose masterpiece was the dome for Florence Cathedral. This great church had been designed in the Middle Ages with a dome, but no one had any conception of how it might be realized. It was only when an open competition was held in 1419 that Brunelleschi stepped forward with a viable solution. His dome was actually two shells of brick, one inside the other, linked together by ribs of brick and strengthened by wooden chains. His greatest breakthrough, however, was to devise a way in which the dome could be constructed without centering, which would have been prohibitively expensive.[4]

The next largest dome built before St Paul's was that of St Peter's in Rome. Mimicking the structure of Brunelleschi's example, this too was steeply pitched and consisted of two shells closely linked by ribs, only this time it was cut entirely in stone. It is a dome of massive proportions, so large in fact that the whole dome of St Paul's, including its lantern, could fit inside it.[5]

A drawing produced by Wren's office and possibly dating from the 1690s directly compares the sections of Florence Cathedral and St Peter's.[6] Wren never went to Italy, so his knowledge of these structures was limited to books. He had, however, been to Paris, where architects were eagerly constructing domes over major public buildings. The Église des Carmes, Église St-Paul-St-Louis, the Sorbonne, the Val-de-Grâce and the Collège des Quatre-Nations all had domes that Wren could have seen on his visit in 1665, and the most impressive, the Val-de-Grâce, was under construction at the time. We can be in no doubt that these examples inspired Wren to consider a dome for St Paul's.[7]

The French domes differed from their Italian counterparts in one important way: the outer dome, visible on the skyline, was made of a timber framework, concealed on the inside by a much lower inner dome made of masonry or plaster. They may have been much less dramatic internally than the great Italian domes, but the French examples had the advantage that they were much quicker and cheaper to construct.

A remarkable set of drawings survives showing how Wren and his office tried a large number of possible configurations for the dome of St Paul's. There are the early and ungainly dome-spires of the pre-Fire and Warrant designs that were loosely based on French precedents. Also belonging to the early period are drawings showing schemes for a Pantheon-like dome. Other drawings looked towards Bramante's Tempietto and Michelangelo's St Peter's in Rome, and Lemercier and

Le Muet's Val-de-Grâce in Paris. There are still further designs that drew heavily upon Les Invalides, constructed long after Wren's trip to France but known to him through copied drawings of the project sent to him by King Charles II in 1678, who had obtained them especially for his architect. In these designs we see Wren struggling on the one hand to reflect the latest fashion and on the other to produce a workable solution within the particular constraints of St Paul's.[8]

The most fundamental problem Wren faced in designing the dome was its weight. By the late 1680s it had become clear that the foundations he had so confidently built were embarrassingly insufficient and that the cathedral was beginning to settle alarmingly. The centre of the building, with its massive piers intended to carry the dome, was considerably heavier than the transepts, choir or nave. Although the whole was sinking slowly into the ground as the weight of building above increased, the central section was sinking faster than the rest. Construction of a heavy masonry dome on top would exacerbate the problem, and if the ground beneath one side of the cathedral turned out to be slightly softer than the other, the results could be catastrophic. It was thus clear that a thick masonry dome of the sort constructed in Florence Cathedral or St Peter's was out of the question. Wren's structure must be very light. It had to be a variant of the French domes, with a thin, lower inner dome, big enough to be impressive from within, and a much larger but cheaper and lighter outer dome in timber to make an impact on the skyline. However, a timber outer dome could have supported only a timber lantern – a rather disappointing element to crown the largest building in the capital, which in any case would have needed frequent repainting or replacing. Wren's solution was ingenious: he designed the first triple dome ever to be constructed.[9]

Double domes – one completely separate dome constructed inside another – had been a popular solution for dome construction for some time. Of the great domes previously constructed, the Pantheon was a

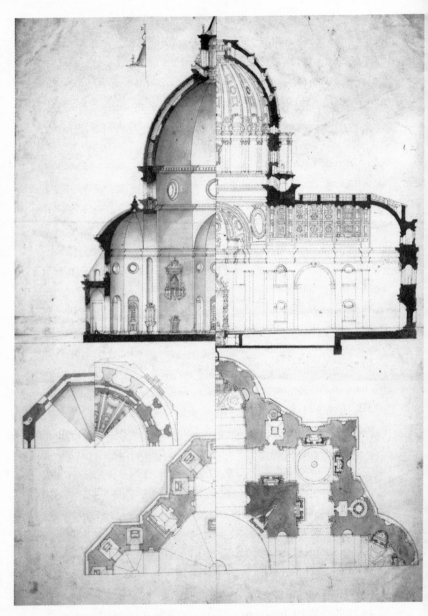

A drawing from Wren's office showing comparative plans and sections of Florence Cathedral (left) and St Peter's in Rome (right).

single concrete shell. Similarly, the dome of Hagia Sophia was not a double dome but a single vault constructed using layers of hollow pots. But St Peter's and Florence Cathedral both had double domes, and they had been used in Persian architecture for centuries. The early fourteenth-century mausoleum of Oljeitu at Sultaniya in Iran had a brick double dome in which the two shells were linked together by ribs in a way strikingly similar to Brunelleschi's solution. (Built only a few decades before, it may have been known in Italy through trading connections.) Nevertheless, all these earlier examples have little in common with Wren's solution, which is entirely novel and based more on science than on architectural precedent.[10]

Looking up from the floor of the central crossing, the observer first sees the inner dome. This is a thin, roughly hemispherical shell 18 inches (46 cm) thick – the length of two standard bricks. In addition, special bricks each 18 inches long were employed in binding courses spaced at regular intervals to hold the two layers of brickwork together. At the dome's centre is an oculus 20 feet (6 m) in diameter. The inner dome was at one time accessible to the public, so a wooden platform and a plain iron balustrade were provided around the oculus (see p. 136).[11]

The stone lantern is supported on a brick cone, the top of which can be seen through the oculus from below. This arrangement had an archi-tectural precedent in the Baptistery at Pisa, though whether Wren knew this or not is uncertain. The cone at St Paul's is constructed of 18-inch brickwork like the inner dome, but is subdivided at intervals with stone bands that contain embedded iron chains. Stone corbels set in these bands at regular intervals hold the ends of the horizontal timber beams that support the dome. The cone measures 94 feet 6 inches (28.8 m) in height, while the stone lantern, which it supports, is 88 feet (26.8 m) high, 16 feet (4.9 m) in diameter at its base, and weighs approximately 700 tons.[12]

In 1708, when Christopher Wren and Edward Strong met on top of the lantern to lay the last stone, the brick cone was exposed to the elements and the lantern must have looked very peculiar, suspended in the air on such an apparently flimsy support. The outer dome that we see today had yet to be constructed. Its body consists of a timber framework of vertical posts and holding horizontal beams that rest on corbels flanking the brick cone. The skin of the dome is made up of vertical timber ribs supporting a framework of horizontal common rafters, which in turn hold the boards to which the lead is nailed.[13]

Domes of brick or stone are normally built on timber centering. Brunelleschi had avoided centering altogether in Florence Cathedral by using a ingenious method of laying the bricks, but Wren had no way of knowing how Brunelleschi's method worked, and in any case had to make a dome that was far lighter and thinner than his Italian counterpart's. Wren did use centering for the inner dome, but it must have been relatively lightweight since it did not reach down to the ground. To achieve this he had to be certain that the dome could carry its own weight – many thousands of tons – as it went up. Traditional lime mortars took months, if not years, to develop their full strength, meaning that the centering would have had to remain in place to prevent the structures below from buckling. The alternative was to find a quicker-drying mortar. Wren experimented with lime mortar made from cockle shells: they produced a good, hard mortar, which he used for plastering the underside of the vaults. It did not dry particularly quickly, however, so for the dome he turned to gypsum, which he knew as plaster of Paris.[14]

The use of gypsum in the construction of domes has a long history in the Middle East, particularly in Persia. Pure gypsum mortar dries extremely fast, so that the mason can hold a brick or tile in place for the few seconds it takes for the mortar to set, and there is no need for any formwork at all. The use of gypsum mortar in vaults constructed with flat tiles rather than oblong bricks was widespread in Spain from the sixteenth century, particularly in the north, and by the nineteenth century the technology had become known as Catalan, or timbrel,

A section through the cathedral drawn by Samuel Swayle and John Gwynn (1755), showing the triple-dome structure.

vaulting. This particular technique had never been widely used in Northern Europe, however.[15]

Wren did not use pure gypsum mortar, but instead combined the gypsum with lime mortar in order to improve its setting properties, thus hoping to have the best of both: a fast-drying mortar that needed little formwork but was also waterproof (the dome would be exposed to the elements until the timber and lead outer roof had been completed). The gypsum came from alabaster quarried in Chellaston, near Derby, and from Tutbury Castle, Staffordshire. Some 244 tons were used during the works.[16]

The structure of the dome also relied on a number of iron chains, embedded within the stonework at regular intervals to resist the outward 'hoop stresses'. The most famous of these is the so-called Great Chain, which is embedded where the base of the cone and the inner dome join the drum of the peristyle; but this is just one of many chains, to be found in external cornices, in the pediment at the west end, in the library cornices and at other points throughout the fabric. Iron generally came in ingots that could be used to make bars of a maximum length of about 16 feet (4.9 m). These long bars, square in section, were formed into chain links and joined together by smaller loops – work all carried out by the Master Ironworker, Thomas Robinson. But equally important as the manufacture of the chains was the way in which they were embedded in the stonework. Individual blocks were dovetailed to slot together and chased with grooves to take the iron. Corrosion would result in failure, since rusting iron would expand and crack the stonework. Wren had noted the failure of iron in repairs to other cathedrals and was generally suspicious of its use, so he had each piece of ironwork completely encased in lead.[17]

Whether Wren determined the position of these chains and the shape of the domes by intuition or by calculation has been the subject of a great deal of discussion. At the centre of all these debates is Wren's relationship with one of the most intriguing figures in seventeenth-century science, Robert Hooke.

Opposite left Part of the timberwork supporting the outer dome, with the exterior of the brick cone visible on the right.

Opposite right A view inside the brick cone of the dome, showing the gallery surrounding the oculus. This space had originally been open to the public. Note the oval windows, which were intended to be lit by corresponding windows in the outer dome, omitted from the design at a late stage.

16

CATENARY CURVES AND
PARABOLIC CONOIDS

Two of Wren's closest colleagues, Robert Hooke and Nicholas Hawksmoor, had a hand in designing the great dome of St Paul's: Hawksmoor was responsible for drawing it, but Hooke – through his scientific theories concerning arches and domes – may have had an even greater influence on its final shape.

Robert Hooke (1635–1703) was only three years younger than Wren. Like Wren, he was the son of a clergyman, but his father died when he was thirteen years old. Hooke was sent to London to study painting under Sir Peter Lely but he left and went to live with Richard Busby, headmaster of Westminster School. Busby had a reputation for taking in intelligent poor scholars, whom he largely educated himself. Of Hooke's brilliance there could be little doubt: he quickly learnt Latin and Greek and started on Hebrew and several other oriental languages. He is also said to have mastered the first six books of Euclid in a week and the organ in twenty lessons. His music lessons proved useful when he secured himself a place as a chorister at Christ Church, Oxford (no doubt with Busby's help), in 1653–54. Here he met the same scientific circle that Wren moved in: Robert Boyle, Thomas Willis, John Wilkins, Seth Ward, William Petty and John Wallis – men who would eventually found the Royal Society.

Hooke, like Wren, had a tremendous talent for making apparatus, and was employed as a laboratory assistant first by the chemist Thomas Willis and then by Robert Boyle. It was Hooke who made the first vacuum pumps and assisted Boyle in his work on springs and on measuring the weight of air. Hooke was the intellectual equal, if not superior, of anyone in his circle; but he was prone to fits of outrage and indignation, and during the course of his career would insult and alienate many, most notably Isaac Newton. Indeed, his argument with Newton was so hostile on both sides that Newton refused to attend the Royal Society until after Hooke's death. When he did so and was elected its president, he made sure that Hooke's portrait was not kept in its collection.[1]

Whatever his shortcomings in character, Hooke was without doubt one of the greatest scientists of his generation. He became the first curator of the Royal Society in London in 1662, and during its early years he was very much responsible for its programme. It was Hooke, on the instruction of the Fellows, who each week made the apparatus, tested it and carried out the demonstrations. The Great Fire of London gave Hooke a second line of employment. He was appointed one of the City's surveyors and was responsible for setting out the boundaries of plots of land before they could be built on and generally for making sure that people were obeying the new building regulations. He was also made Professor of Geometry at Gresham College in 1665, where he lived until his death.[2]

Hooke scrupulously described his hectic commitments in his diary, which provides an invaluable record of his life and of those around him. Wren makes frequent appearances, and it is clear that they were close friends (Hooke, for example, once gave Wren a hobby horse to mark his son's birthday). The two men met up frequently, partly to discuss science and partly to talk about architecture. Hooke helped Wren with the planning of the City churches, apparently making drawings of, and perhaps even designing, a handful of churches himself, although no doubt only under the close scrutiny of Wren. From his college rooms in Bishopsgate (only ten minutes' walk from St Paul's) Hooke could easily visit the construction sites as he went about his other duties. This and his surveying work brought Hooke into regular contact with tradesmen of all kinds, and his diaries record numerous evenings spent in taverns conversing with them. Indeed, it was this willingness – shared by Wren – to meet such men on equal terms that engendered their mutual respect and cooperation. It was Hooke's ideas about arches and domes, however, that had particular significance for the design of St Paul's.[3]

The 'correct' shape for arches was first discussed at the Royal Society at one of its weekly afternoon meetings, on 8 December 1670. On this particular occasion the president, William Brouncker, was in the chair. The minutes record how

> Mr Hooke brought in this problem of architecture: The basis of the distance of two pillars and the altitude of an arch being given, to find out the right figure for that arch, for the firm sustaining, upon the whole, or any part of it, any weight given; as also to find out the abutments of that arch. Mr Hooke being asked, whether he had a demonstration of this useful problem, he said he had it, and would show it to the President.[4]

This 'demonstration' was what we would now call a mathematical 'proof'. A week later, on 15 December, Hooke presented a working model illustrating his hypothesis:

> Mr Hooke represented the mechanical way of making an arch of such a figure, as shall sustain any weight given. Being asked, whether he had the demonstration [mathematical proof] of it, he answered that he had given it to the President, who was absent from the meeting.[5]

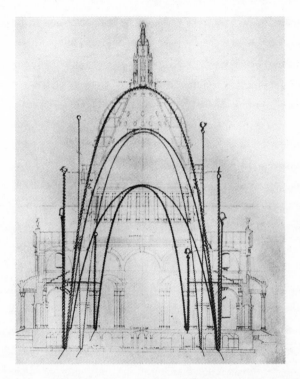

An early twentieth-century attempt to superimpose an inverted image of hanging chains on a drawing of St Paul's. The match is remarkably good for the inner dome, but no weight has been placed on the outer chain to simulate the weight of the outer dome, so it falls well outside the cone.

It seems likely Hooke was fibbing, hoping that he could work out the solution over Christmas. As it happened, he never reached the mathematical solution, but five years later, in 1675, he did reveal his hypothesis. To avoid others stealing the idea and solving it before him, he published it as an anagram in Latin in his book on helioscopes; he also wrote it in his diary. This method of publishing the hypotheses of half-finished problems in code or anagrams – so that, if asked, the author could prove that he had had the idea first – was popular at the time. When deciphered, Hooke's hypothesis read: *Ut pendet continuum flexile, sic stabit contiguum rigidum inversum*: 'As hangs the flexible line, so but inverted will stand the rigid arch.'[6]

Hooke's theory – that the perfect shape for a thin arch is that formed by a hanging chain, but inverted – is correct. All one has to do is find a chain of the appropriate length and weight and hang it from two correctly spaced supports. The resulting curve, once inverted, is the best shape for the arch. Adjusting the length of the chain alters the height of the arch, and the longer the chain, the less the outward force exerted on the abutments. The shape thus formed is ideal for a uniformly loaded arch, but point loads can be simulated by hanging appropriately sized weights from the chains at the relevant points. It is probably this sort of model that Hooke had presented to the Royal Society on 15 December 1670.

Hooke's failure to provide a mathematical equation describing the catenary (the shape of a hanging flexible chain) was not on account of any laziness on his part: the mathematical methods involved were simply not yet available. The solution required calculus, which Newton and Leibniz would invent independently around this time, but was not published or understood by others until later. Indeed, even once armed with calculus, the problem of devising an equation for the catenary challenged some of the greatest mathematicians of the age, including Daniel Bernoulli, Christiaan Huygens and Leibniz himself.[7]

Crucially Hooke's method did not need a mathematical solution: his great insight was that the shape could be obtained by the use of models such as a simple hanging chain, which could be adjusted to test various possible solutions. Hooke's diary for Saturday 5 June 1675 records: 'At Sir Chr. Wren … He was making up my principle about arches and altered his module [design] by it.' This has been taken to mean that Wren altered his designs for the dome at this point, but Hooke mentions only arches. The dome was almost certainly designed using Hooke's principles, but not for at least another decade; and a dome entailed a slightly different set of considerations, which Hooke had already examined separately. He demonstrated his theory of domes at the Royal Society on 7 December 1671, a year after his demonstration of the principle of the arch:[8]

Mr Hooke produced the representation of the figure of the arch of a cupola for the sustaining such and such determinate weights, and found it to be a cubico-parabolic conoid; adding that by this figure might be determined all the difficulties in architecture about arches and abutments. He was desired to bring the demonstration and description of it in writing to be registered.[9]

A cubico-parabolic conoid is the curve produced by flipping the curve of a $y=x^3$ graph around the y-axis. It is now clear that this is not the best shape for a masonry dome, but the problem was still being debated as late as the twentieth century. What is interesting is that Hooke links the

Recent research by Gordon Higgott has demonstrated that Wren used the idea of a cubico-parabolic conoid to produce the curve of the dome in this drawing for St Paul's.

problem to his discoveries surrounding arches. Perhaps he felt that the curve $y=x^3$ fitted the catenary, in which case he was mistaken. In practice, domes are different from arches because of their three dimensional rotation. This leads to problems with outward thrusts in the lower area of the dome; but at the crown there is no stress at all, so the masonry can be safely omitted at this point without weakening the structure. This is what happens at the Pantheon and elsewhere, including numerous examples at St Paul's where oculi are introduced to let light in.[10]

One of the later drawings for the brick cone shows Wren toying with the $y=x^3$ shape, but it seems more likely that he used the idea of the catenary to form the arches that make up his inner dome, simply revolving them through 360 degrees and simplifying them where necessary.[11] The brick cone that Wren actually built is not part of a catenary or a cubico-parabolic conoid: it is simply a straight-sided cone with the top removed. It was easier to build that way, but it also approximates the shape a hanging chain will make if a very large weight (simulating the stone lantern) is hung at its middle. Similarly, the inner dome is very close to the shape an unweighted chain might make, which in turn is close to a hemisphere with its centre removed. Both domes rest on the peristyle, which has sloping sides to spread the load.

Wren did not leave anything to chance. In October and November 1693 his designs for the dome were built as large-scale models in stone so that they could be properly tested. For all the theorizing and discussion, it was probably models such as these that determined the dome's final form. Structural mechanics was in its infancy and it was not yet possible to use mathematics alone to calculate whether a masonry building would stand up. While theories might help in suggesting novel solutions, Wren and his masons were forced to rely on physical models and established practice. In that respect at least, their methods were not greatly different from those of the medieval masons who preceded them.[12]

17

THE TELESCOPE IN THE TOWER

In the period 1702–11, as construction of the dome progressed, the west end of the cathedral also began to take shape, including the famous two-storey portico with its twin towers (Plate 8). Although little comment appeared in print, we know from *Parentalia*, in which Christopher Wren junior felt it necessary to defend his father's design, that the architect's decision to divide the portico into two storeys was much criticized. He claimed that Wren had originally intended a single giant order of columns, but it had not been possible to obtain stones from Portland large enough to make the shafts. The change to columns of a smaller diameter limited their height, since in Classical architecture the relationship between the two is fixed, and he had thus been obliged to include two storeys. Wren's final design also reflected the latest advances in French architecture introduced in Claude Perrault's recently completed east front for the Louvre.[1]

Flanking the west portico on either side are the two towers. Earlier drawings had shown each tower surmounted by a two-storey circular temple seemingly inspired by Bramante's Tempietto, which was widely illustrated in the architectural literature of the time. But Wren had placed a statue on the top of each dome – something that certainly does not feature in Bramante's original.[2]

The official view of the proposed west front, engraved by Simon Gribelin, approved by Wren and published in 1702. At this stage, the west towers were surmounted by simple lanterns based on Bramante's Tempietto. The upper dome also differs from that executed.

A wooden model for the design of a tower (perhaps the one discussed above) appears to have been made in 1700 by the joiner John Smallwell, at the cost of £13. In September 1701 Smallwell was paid again, this time 'For 52 days 1 man Altering the Modell of one of the Towers at the W End, to show the Winding Staires & Raising it higher & Making ye corners square which were hollow before at 3s per day £7 16s'. In subsequent drawings the Tempietto-inspired top was raised on a plinth; one drawing shows the plinth with windows, but sometime later it was altered again to allow for clock faces to be inserted on all four sides. This is the façade shown in the engraving by Simon Gribelin that Wren officially approved for publication in 1702, but it was not the design that was built. Indeed, there seems to have been considerable uncertainty surrounding the design of the top of the towers: yet another model of the tower was made in January 1706, this time in stone; and then two more stone models of the tops of the towers in January and June 1707.[3]

Although they are identical on the outside, the two towers are not the same internally (a fact that possibly accounts for the two separate models of them built in 1707). That on the north-west is the bell tower and contains various rooms within it. The south-west tower, which is the clock tower, is hollow. Inside, the lower section consists of an enormous stone shaft, 24 feet (7.3 m) in diameter and over 100 feet (30 m) high. An oculus in the centre of the domed ceiling high above is now obscured by the clock, but originally it would allowed glimpses through to the stone vault some 80 feet above that. A precipitous staircase winds up around the outside of the shaft, providing access to the triforium level.

There is evidence to suggest that Wren may have intended to use this tall space for scientific experiments. Back in 1664 Hooke had carried out experiments on barometric pressure and very long pendulums while balanced precariously in the upper reaches of Old St Paul's, which he measured as being 204 feet (62 m) high. Scholars have recently suggested that this stairwell in the new cathedral was also intended for a scientific endeavour, mentioned in documents in 1704: the use of the whole tower as a giant zenith telescope.[4]

Most people understand a telescope to be a long tube – either held by hand or mounted on a frame of some sort – for viewing far-away objects. The only difference between a standard telescope and a zenith telescope is that the latter is fixed vertically, so that it can only look straight up. Theoretically, this has the advantage that a much longer telescope should be possible, because the frame can be made completely rigid; and the longer the telescope, the greater the magnification. During the seventeenth century there had been much progress in the grinding of lenses, which allowed the use of telescopes of a very long focal length. The zenith telescope thus represented the very latest in astronomical technology and theoretically made the measurement of stellar parallax – minute movements in a star's position occasioned by the earth's orbit around the sun – possible to a degree of accuracy hitherto unimagined.[5]

The obvious disadvantage of the zenith telescope is that it cannot be aimed. The observer has to wait for the earth to move and for stars to come into view directly above it. If the weather is inclement on the evening when a particular object is due to enter the field of view, the observation cannot be made and the opportunity is lost.

Wren and Hooke had already made at least one previous attempt to construct a zenith telescope. In 1676 they had built one inside the Monument commemorating the Great Fire of London. The Monument took the form of a giant column, similar to – and inspired by – Trajan's Column in Rome. They had constructed it to be hollow, with a small, dark observational laboratory in the basement and a mechanism for opening a hole in the decoration on top. Both features survive to this day. Their attempts at making observations, however, were unsuccessful – a situation they attributed to movements in the slender tower caused by wind and by traffic. Neither this failure nor Hooke's death in 1703 seems to have diminished Wren's enthusiasm for the enterprise.[6]

In February 1704, at the Council of the Royal Society, Wren suggested that St Paul's could be used to house a zenith telescope, which would incorporate lenses donated to the Society by Constantijn Huygens (elder brother of the virtuoso scientist Christiaan) in 1692 along with 'the Apparatus for using them without a Tube'. It is not clear, however, where exactly in the cathedral he wanted to install them. The idea that they were destined for the tower comes from the fact that this was being constructed at the time, and from a reference in John Ward's *Lives of the Gresham Professors*:[7]

> Sir Christopher Wren designed to make use of the hollow of the great staircase on the south side, being in height 96 feet 11 inches, for the like purpose as the Monument, by the assistance of the great telescope presented to the Royal Society by Mr Huygens; and his kinsman, the ingenious mathematician, Mr James Hodgson was to have made the observations. But finding the instrument, which is 123 feet long, too large for his use, and not being able to procure any other of a proper size, he was prevented likewise from the execution of that design.[8]

The 'great staircase on the south side' mentioned here has been taken to mean the Dean's stair in the south-west tower. But if that is so, Ward's account is slightly puzzling: the interior of the south-west tower, if the upper spire is included, is in fact much taller than 123 feet (37.5 m), the supposed length of the telescope. There are two possible reasons why the telescope was not built. First, the telescope may have required a space that matched the focal length of the lenses more or less exactly, since the lenses had to be firmly mounted to the structure itself. If that was the case, the focal length of Huygens's lenses would not have been too big for the south-west tower, merely the wrong size, meaning that they would have had to be suspended in mid air. The other explanation is that the staircase in question was not, as has been assumed, in the south-west tower at all, but rather the Great Stair on the south side of the cathedral, which had been used throughout the works to carry goods up and down and which now forms the main access for visitors to the cathedral's upper levels. At the centre of this staircase is a huge, dark stone shaft that now houses a lift, but in 1704 it would have been empty and ideal for a telescope. Measured drawings show it to have been about 97 feet (29.5 m) tall.[9]

What is clear, however, is that no suitable space was found, and the idea of using the cathedral as a telescope was subsequently abandoned. A clock now covers the hole above the Dean's stair, preventing any view of the sky, and the roof over the Great Stair similarly blocks the view. Whether or not it was used as a telescope, the south-west tower contains one feature that is undoubtedly unusual: the Dean's stair.

Astronomical considerations aside, the staircase in the south-west tower is a most remarkable piece of architecture. The stair itself, which rises from ground to triforium gallery level in the south-west tower, is known as the 'Dean's stair' since it was designed to give the dean access to his library (the Deanery is a hundred yards south of this tower). Why such a dramatic staircase should have been necessary for such a mundane purpose is not clear, but the staircase that was constructed is one of the most impressive spaces in the entire cathedral. It consists of two flights. The lowest is 6 feet (1.8 m) wide and rises from outside ground level to the level of the floor of the cathedral, where a landing connects with a door in the southern vestibule. The second flight then rises eighty-eight steps up to the triforium gallery without encountering any type of landing along the way. Its steps, which are 4 feet (1.2 m) in width, are only a few inches thick and appear to cantilever precariously from the walls, forming one of the longest continuous flights of cantilever stairs in the world.

Sometimes also called the 'Geometrical stair', the Dean's stair belongs to a type of staircase that had exercised a considerable fascination for Renaissance architects. Palladio had published a number of examples of cantilevered stairs in his *Quattro libri dell'architettura* (1570), designed in circular, elliptical and square stairwells, along with a particularly complicated double-helical version. These plates have led some writers to name the type the 'Palladian stair', but this is a misnomer. Palladio used many other styles of staircase in his buildings and he certainly did not invent the form (there are examples from antiquity). There is little question, however, that it was Palladio's books that provided the inspiration for early English examples. One of the first in Britain is the dramatic cantilever stair set in a rectangular well at the Queen's House in Greenwich, designed by Inigo Jones and completed in the 1630s.[10]

One of the unusual features of the St Paul's staircase was its mode of construction. With this type of stair, each tread would normally be fitted in place as the walls were constructed. This ensured that the tread was firmly anchored into the masonry and also minimizes the need for scaffolding. However, during repairs carried out in 2005 it became clear that the stair had not been built in this way. Initially only the shaft seems to have been constructed, with no allowance made for cutting in the stairs. Wren approved a model for the staircase in February 1704, but it was not until September that work began on cutting holes into the smooth shaft, into which the steps could be slotted. The south door was modified at the same time, suggesting that it had not originally been intended as a major entrance. Once the holes had been cut, William Kempster carved the stairs, completing them by May 1705. Each step was slotted precisely into the hole made for it, so that it bears directly onto the one beneath, and it was held in place by slim metal wedges driven into the wall above each tread and concealed in the mortar.[11]

There is still considerable debate among engineers surrounding the structural properties of stairs of this kind. It is generally agreed that they

A view up the shaft of the Dean's stair, in the south-west tower.

do not cantilever out of the wall (and thus should not strictly be called 'cantilever stairs') but rely instead on loads being transferred along the bottom edges of each tread onto the one beneath. The narrower this contact point, the more daring the stair. The wall does help to carry some of the load, but mainly it stops the step rotating. This explains how very long (and thus very heavy stairs) can be built into apparently poorly constructed brick or stone walls without any obvious ill effects. When failure does occur, it is mostly at landings, which may be one reason why Wren chose not to include any intermediate landings here.[12]

Stairs of this sort are vulnerable to any tiny movements of the wall, which turned out to be a problem at St Paul's. If something softer than the stone itself had been used to wedge each tread in place, the material might have absorbed some of the pressure; but as the wall settled, the metal wedges could not take up the movement and simply dug into the stone, leading to dramatic cracks in some of the treads. Subsequent rusting of the iron made the cracking worse, necessitating the restoration undertaken in 2005.[13]

The reason behind the late insertion of the treads in the south-west tower remains a mystery. There is no doubt that Wren had originally intended to build stairs here; but he may have been asked to omit them when funds were uncertain, only to reinsert them later when a steady income was more secure. Alternatively, being undecided between a single stair and a double stair, Wren may have chosen to keep his options open; or he may simply have been waiting for the building to settle. Whatever the case, the geometrical stairs remain one of the most dramatic, puzzling and delightful features of the whole cathedral.

The treads of the Dean's stair, with wrought-iron balustrades by Jean Tijou.

18

FRAUDS AND ABUSES

Up until the year 1709, through three decades of the cathedral's construction, Wren had been on good terms with the commission. In the early years the commissioners had been distracted chiefly by the challenge of finding enough money to continue the work, and the committee minutes suggest that they took little interest in the design. In fact, Wren is recorded as having shown the building sub-committee plans or drawings on only four occasions in thirty-five years: once in 1676, twice in 1693, and once more in 1700. On each occasion they had specifically asked to see them. It was only with the introduction of the new extended Coal Tax in 1702, when the finances ceased to be a problem, that the commissioners could turn their attention to the cathedral's design. It may have been this, or the personalities involved, that led to the subsequent souring of relations between Wren and his employers. Details of the resulting scandals are extremely complicated and need not concern us here, but it is worth recounting at least some of the stories, since they are very revealing of seventeenth-century building practice.[1]

The first problems arose in 1709, over negotiations for a contract to produce iron railings to enclose the cathedral and its yard. Up to this point the ironwork at St Paul's had been supplied by a number of contractors. The day-to-day ironmongery – which included bolts, spikes,

hinges and the great chains embedded in the masonry – had been supplied by Thomas Robinson and Thomas Coalburne up until 1704, and
thereafter by Robinson alone. The decorative work, which included the
ironwork in the windows, had been made by perhaps the greatest ironworker of the age, Jean Tijou.[2]

Tijou is a mysterious character. We know that he was French, but
beyond that we have tantalizingly little information surrounding his life
and career, apart from brief mentions in building accounts and letters.
It has been suggested that he was a Huguenot who sought refuge first in
the Netherlands and then came over to England with William and Mary.
Tijou's works for Wren included Hampton Court, Kensington Palace
and Greenwich Hospital. In all these cases his ironwork showed an
extraordinary delicacy and originality of design. Since he was already
engaged on St Paul's (and would continue to be so until 1711), Tijou was
the natural choice to supply the new railings. His prices were reasonable
and the quality of his work beyond reproach. It was therefore peculiar, to
say the least, that the contract should be given to Richard Jones, an
unknown contractor with no track record in producing ironwork.[3]

It is unclear exactly how Richard Jones managed to convince the
commissioners that he was the right person to produce the railings,
although it later became apparent that he was an unsavoury character,
and it is quite possible he had some mysterious hold over one or more of
them. It was certainly not at Wren's suggestion.

When the subject of the fence first arose, Jones persuaded the commission that he should be allowed to submit an estimate for the railings,
which he duly did at a meeting on 3 March 1709. It was clear from the
outset that Jones did not intend to make the railings himself: he was only a
go-between, acting as agent for a Mr Gott who ran an ironworks in
Sussex. This may immediately have angered the other contractors and
aroused the Surveyor's suspicions, for all the other contractors at St Paul's
were responsible for carrying out the work themselves. Jones's suggestion

that the railings should be erected in cast iron rather than wrought iron was also a concern: it was a most unusual use of cast iron at the time, and in fact the railings remain one of the earliest recorded uses of architectural cast iron. Jones argued that using this material would ensure their longevity. The commission was convinced, but Wren was not. Indeed, the Surveyor argued that Jones's estimate was far too high and that other contractors should be approached. Nothing Wren could say made any difference, however: a vote was taken at a meeting on 28 January 1710 and he was defeated. Thereafter, Wren's dealings with the commissioners seem to have become increasingly acrimonious, while their treatment of him was seen by his loyal craftsmen as nothing short of scandalous. Wren himself might have ignored the slight had it not been for the case that was brought against Richard Jenings.[4]

Between 1700 and 1710 the great dome steadily rose above the rest of the cathedral. The work depended on the ingenuity of the Master Carpenter, who was responsible for devising and building the formwork upon which the inner dome and cone would be constructed, and then for providing the final outer structure of timber that formed the dome visible on the London skyline. At this time the position was occupied by Richard Jenings, whose rise from apprentice to head carpenter at St Paul's was noted in Chapter 10.

Entries detailing the scaffolding for the stonework of the dome dominate the carpentry accounts for 1704. In February 1705 the carpenters were building centering for the dome's architrave. The first great centres for the internal brick dome were set up in May 1705, and scaffolding work continued inside and outside the dome throughout the rest of 1705, 1706 and for most of 1707. In May 1707 Jenings was busy directing the carpenters in their framing of the permanent timberwork for the great outer dome on the ground, although it would not be raised into position until early 1709. By the middle of 1708 the other roofs were all completed and boarded ready for the plumbers. By the end of 1709 the dome itself was finished and much of the scaffolding inside it was being taken down.

During the period 1705–10 Jenings had overseen between eighty and one hundred carpenters on site every month. This in itself was remarkable, but he had also been responsible for the erection of an ingenious flying scaffold that allowed the bricklayers to build the dome at great height without the need for a structure rising from the floor. In December 1706 Jenings received a payment of £53 15*s.* (or 50 guineas) 'For his Skill and Extraordinary Pains, Care & Diligence in the performance of the Centering of the Dome & for the models of the same'. The exact form this scaffolding took is lost and there is too little information in the accounts for it to be reconstructed. The only description we possess is a brief paragraph in *Parentalia*:[5]

> The great Colonade that encircles the Dome without, serves for the Butment of the [inner] dome, which is Brick of two Bricks thick, but as it rises every five feet high, has a Course of excellent Bricks of 18 inches long, banding through the whole thickness. (a) The Concave was turned upon a Centre; which was judged necessary to keep the Worke even and true, tho' a Cupola might be built without a Centre; but this is observable, that the Centre was laid without any standards from below to support it; and as it was both Centering and Scaffolding, it remained for use of the Painter. Every Story of this Scaffolding being circular, and the Ends of the Ledgers, meeting as many Rings, and truly wrought, it supported itself.[6]

Aside from being a brilliant carpenter, Jenings was also an outspoken individual and unwaveringly loyal to Wren. He was openly critical of the way the commissioners had treated the Surveyor over the appointment of Richard Jones and took every opportunity to say so in public. He was equally vehement in his condemnation of Jones, who was proving slow in producing the railings, which Wren felt were inferior in quality.[7]

Jenings had come across two revealing facts about Jones. The first was that he had been branded on the hand for his part in a manslaughter. As far as Jenings was concerned, this made him a common criminal. The second was that he had previously been prosecuted for fraud. Both were true: Jones had been involved in a riot and had been tried and convicted, along with a number of others, of the manslaughter of a man they had beaten to death. He had also been tried for changing a contract, although he managed to get off on a technicality.[8]

What Jenings probably did not know, but which emerged later, was that Jones was diverting much of the money he was allocated for the railings at St Paul's to pay off his son's tax debts. Since these amounted to some £6,000 and the overall cost of the fence was £11,000, it is clear with hindsight that Jones was defrauding the cathedral of a huge sum of money. It seems, however, that Jones had protectors within the commission (no doubt the same men who had secured him the job). Certainly, the commission would not tolerate any criticism of its actions in general, nor of its employment of Jones in particular. They set out to punish Jenings for his insolence and to make it clear that anything less than absolute obedience would not be tolerated.[9]

In 1710 Jenings's work was nearing completion and he began to lay off men. Most must have been expecting this, but undoubtedly there were some who were aggrieved by it. The commissioners saw their opportunity, managing to persuade some of the dismissed men to accuse their former master of embezzlement.[10]

The first charges brought against him were serious and also the most interesting. Wren had insisted from the outset that the carpenters be paid by the day to ensure that there were always enough of them on site to carry out the work quickly. The Master Carpenter was paid 3s. a day and received 2*s*. 6*d*. per day for each of the workmen below him. The accusation was that Jenings had paid his workmen less than 2*s*. 6*d*. and pocketed the difference; that he was paid seven days a week but was not on site every day; and that he collected money for elderly and infirm carpenters who should not have been employed at all. Jenings was summoned on 13 September 1710 to appear before the commissioners at the next meeting and to explain his conduct.[11]

Jenings's defence given at the meeting held on 20 September 1710 was straightforward and revealing. First, he admitted that he did indeed pay his men less than he received for them, but maintained that there was nothing underhand in this: it was simply normal practice. Second, he reminded the commission that his allowance was paid for seven days a week according to custom, as it had been to his predecessors; and that he often came in on Sundays and holidays to look after the site, even keeping lodgings on site to enable him to do so. As far as the last charge was concerned, Jenings admitted that he did indeed employ some who were elderly or had been injured, but this was a charitable act owed to long-serving workers, who in any event were employed doing jobs that otherwise would need to be done by able-bodied men. Furthermore, he noted that if he had done the work 'by Great', he would have made more profit by it. Wren supported Jenings in all his replies and pointed out that his work was outstanding and excellent value for money. He would later repeat all these comments in writing.[12]

The commissioners were forced to back down, but they were not happy. Despite Wren's protests, they voted at the same meeting to pay Jones £1,000 as a part sum for the fence, directly overruling the Surveyor, who claimed that Jones's work was substandard. It seems to have been one insult too far, and one that the elderly Surveyor could not tolerate. Thereafter he would distance himself from the commission's decisions. He would continue to act as Surveyor, but he decided he would not attend any more commissioners' meetings.[13]

By February 1711 the commission had found more disgruntled carpenters willing to testify against Jenings. Two of his senior carpenters, George Purchase and Thomas Hill, prevented the witnesses from putting their case before the commission and were dismissed from the works for their insolence in March 1711, when a new case was put together. This time the commission accused Jenings not only of embezzling money, but also of stealing goods from the cathedral works and of getting his men to sign in at St Paul's while they were being paid to work elsewhere. Again, Jenings answered the case convincingly. He produced a signed affidavit from sixty of his carpenters to the effect that the accusations were false, and he invited the commissioners to examine the account books and call books themselves. It was to no avail. The commissioners summarily dismissed him from the works on 14 April. John James was appointed to succeed him on a salary of £200 (a figure set deliberately to match Wren's) on the understanding that henceforth the Master Carpenter would pay his men directly without deductions from the money given to him.[14]

The commissioners pursued other complaints of corruption during this period, but the case against Jenings is particularly important because of the insight it gives into the way workmen were paid. There is no reason to doubt the veracity of Jenings's claim that it was normal practice at the time for overseers to deduct a portion of the money they received to cover their own costs. After all, they often had to wait for payment. Normally this deduction would have been modest and would probably not have attracted interest, but owing to the number of carpenters on site during the construction of the dome, Jenings was being paid very large sums of money indeed. The commissioners calculated that personally he was making £1,500 per year during this period – an exaggeration. Nevertheless, the accounts for the period 1707–10 show that he did make a total personal profit, after he had paid his men, of somewhere between £2,830 and £5,446, which was certainly a very considerable sum of money, the equivalent of several million pounds in modern currency. One can begin to see why the commissioners were angry.[15]

The matter was not completely over, however. On 17 October 1711 the commission received a letter from the attorney general demanding that Jenings be prosecuted. The commission may have thought their luck was in, but in fact Wren had been manoeuvring behind the scenes. Nine months earlier he had written to the archbishop of Canterbury and the bishop of London asking for the remainder of his salary, which was being held back from him until the cathedral was finished. Wren claimed that the cathedral's completion was out of his control. He said that the commission had ignored his comments regarding the iron fence and the inner dome, which they had decided to have painted quite contrary to his instructions. Since he was thus effectively no longer in charge, he asked that he might therefore be given the money that was owed to him. In February Wren followed this up with a submission directly to the House of Commons and two letters to the queen, the latter claiming that the commission was preventing him from erecting the statue she had paid for. In October 1711 he got his wish: to its great surprise, the commission found itself suspended. Furthermore, the attorney general threw out the complaint against Jenings as being without foundation. Parliament agreed that the salary withheld from Wren should be paid, and directed that the cathedral should be declared officially complete on 25 December 1711.[16]

From all this, it would appear that Wren had won. In fact, a series of pamphlets published by both parties had damaged his reputation and caused embarrassment to all. Yet in the short term, at least, Wren was able to continue as Surveyor relatively unhindered.

19

THE CATHEDRAL COMPLETED

On 1 August 1714 Wren's great supporter, Queen Anne, died. Since she had handed control of the cathedral back to Wren in 1711, her statue had been erected in front of the cathedral according to his directions and a fence had been built around it by Tijou. Apart from these cosmetic improvements and some tidying up, little work had been done on the cathedral itself, most of the workers' time and energy being expended on the construction of the Chapter House, for which Wren employed Jenings – presumably as a direct snub to the dean and the commissioners. No work was carried out on the painting of the dome, or any other changes the Surveyor had objected to. He ignored John James, whom the commission had nominally appointed as Master Carpenter and who wrote to the Earl of Oxford to complain that he was out of pocket.[1]

But with Queen Anne's death and the accession of George I, a Whig government came to power once more and a new commission was formed. It met for the first time on 25 June 1715. Many of its members were the same as before, but there were some new additions, most notably Sir Isaac Newton. Although he attended a number of times in 1715, Newton was obviously bored by the proceedings and does not appear thereafter.[2]

One of the first items of business was the formation of a new subcommittee to look into the Frauds and Abuses case that by now had been so well aired in published pamphlets. On 28 June the commission met again and confirmed Wren's reappointment as Surveyor, but with John James as his assistant. More importantly, they directed that the dome should be painted forthwith, according to designs prepared by Sir James Thornhill. We are not sure in what way Wren intended to complete the centrepiece of his design, but he seems to have preferred a formal pattern of painted coffers rather than the scenes depicting the life of St Paul that were actually created. The following week, on 2 July 1715, the commissioners met once more and asked Wren and the new Assistant Surveyor to produce an estimate for the completion of the works, directing that no workmen should be employed without their approval. It was the last meeting Wren attended. Finding the commission much as it had been before, he decided to take no further part in the proceedings. He remained nominally the Surveyor until his death and the commission seems to have been gracious enough not to deprive him of this title; but from the minutes it is clear that he had ceased to act as such, and that John James had effectively taken over, under the close direction of the commission. Wren was now eighty-three years old and unwilling to fight. Without his involvement, the commission set about completing the cathedral to their satisfaction. This included ordering the glazing in of the lantern, the painting of the dome, and the erection of a balustrade around the top of the cathedral.[3]

The lantern on the top of the dome had initially been unglazed, but water was dripping onto the floor of the cathedral when it rained. Wren can hardly have objected to the practical decision to glaze it, but he strongly opposed the inclusion of Thornhill's paintings on the inside of the dome. As far as the construction of a balustrade was concerned, Wren's early Warrant design had included such a feature, but since then his elevations had terminated in a plain upstand, or plinth, above the cornice, which he had already completed. The commissioners decided (perhaps on advice) that it required further embellishment, and thus directed John James to produce a model.[4]

The events that followed have always been presented as a further evidence of the commission's disgraceful conduct towards the Surveyor in his old age. In fact, it is not quite so straightforward. Despite all their previous disagreements, and much to their credit, the commissioners continued to recognise Wren as the Surveyor and to seek his approval for their designs and actions. It was not forthcoming, but it was Wren who seems to have refused to attend meetings despite frequent requests. The commissioners appear to have done everything they could to obtain his assent. First, they sought Isaac Newton's advice on the matter –

Sir James Thornhill's controversial paintings inside the dome.

presumably hoping that Newton was the sort of figure who would command Wren's respect. They requested revised drafts from John James, and asked Newton himself take them to Wren for approval. In 1717 Wren wrote a curt reply, condemning the addition and noting that 'ladies think nothing well without edging'. Having been generally treated with contempt, the commissioners decided to proceed with their design anyway, with John James directing the works.[5]

Of course, it is probable that the commissioners were simply 'going through the motions' and had no intention of backing down, but neither did they ignore Wren entirely. In his letter, Wren had mentioned that statues should be placed only in the pediments and on the plinths he had provided for the purpose. In this, his wishes appear to have been followed. Thornhill's hated paintings for the inside of the dome were completed by September 1721. The carver Francis Bird completed the statuary for the pediment at the west end in 1722, but figures for the north and south transepts were not ordered until 1724, after Wren's death.[6]

Wren's final years saw an enforced retirement from public life. From 1715, the year he withdrew from St Paul's, he found his powers in the Office of the King's Works much reduced. It seems that in his old age he was failing to keep a check on the activities of his subordinates. He was finally ousted from his post as Surveyor of the King's Works by the political scheming of William Benson, who had Wren's patent revoked on 26 April 1718 so that he could take over. Benson proved to be the most incompetent Surveyor in the history of the Office of Works, and his blatant corruption eventually led to his dismissal. To add to the indignity of losing his post, Wren was forced to leave his lodgings in Whitehall. No longer involved in St Paul's or the Office of Works, he retired to the Surveyor's house at Hampton Court overlooking the green, which had been granted to him as a residence for life by Queen Anne. He also owned a house in St James's Street, Westminster, which his son later inherited. How he divided his time between the two residences is uncertain. Since St Paul's was now open to the public, he would have been able visit the cathedral as often as he wished, and officially, of course, he remained in charge.[7]

It is an oft-told story that after visiting the chilly interior of his own cathedral one winter's day, Wren contracted a cold that killed him. Historical documents, however, suggest that he fell ill while travelling from Hampton Court to Westminster. In his old age Wren liked to nap after lunch. On the afternoon of 25 February 1723, at home in St James's, one of Wren's servants thought it strange that he was sleeping longer than usual. He went to Wren's apartment and found the nonagenarian Surveyor, England's greatest architect, slumped dead in his chair.[8]

***

The interior of the cathedral today is not entirely as Wren designed it, nor indeed as it was at the time of his death. One of the most significant departures from the architect's intentions is the series of paintings in the dome – so disliked by Wren – that were completed in 1721. They have not been universally admired, and during the nineteenth century there were even discussions about the possibility of replacing them.[9]

Beneath the dome, the rest of the cathedral was originally relatively plain. The walls were painted up to cornice level with a unifying, greyish stone-coloured paint, while the vaults above were whitewashed to produce a clean and light-filled interior. Only the east end of the choir and the peristyle of the dome interior had any gilding, with the pilasters around the apse being painted blue and veined in gold. The view from the choir into the apse end of the cathedral was unobstructed and remained so into the middle of the nineteenth century.[10]

Since that time a number of changes have been made. It is probably the east end of the cathedral that has altered most. First, the timber screen that housed the organ, dividing the choir from the crossing and the nave, was removed in the 1860s. This opened up a view down the complete length of the cathedral for the first time. In the same period the choir stalls were moved a bay westwards, towards the crossing. Following a large number of different proposals submitted by various artists, the upper walls and vaults of the choir were decorated in lavish mosaics, starting in 1891. This had been a controversial project from the start, and work was halted in 1901 under mounting objections from the art world. Finally, in the Second World War a bomb fell through the roof into the crypt. It failed to explode, but the nineteenth-century high altar was destroyed by the impact, and the bomb left a large hole in the roof and floor. As part of the post-war restoration, the cathedral decided to erect a baldacchino in honour of the design proposed by Wren but rejected so long before. The structure that stands there today is thus an idea of what Wren's original might have been like, dreamt up by an eccentric twentieth-century architect called Stephen Dykes Bower.[11]

As for the rest of the building, the greatest change since Wren's day is the profusion of monuments. With the exception of the delightful monument to John Donne by Nicholas Stone, hidden away in the south choir aisle – the only monument to survive the Great Fire intact and be re-erected in the new cathedral – new sculpture was not placed in the body of the new cathedral until the very end of the eighteenth century. There were monuments, but they were confined to the crypt. Between that date and the end of the First World War, they multiplied.[12]

The celebrated Great Model has had a peripatetic past. Originally placed in the Trophy Room (then known as the North Library), it was lent in 1857 to the South Kensington Museum (now the Victoria and Albert Museum). Upon its return in the 1880s it was left in the corridor outside its original home, finally moving back inside in 1927. In 1982 the model went down to the crypt, to return to its proper place in the Trophy Room only after an exhibition in 1992.[13]

Many of the remaining alterations to St Paul's have been made as a result of changes in use. The Consistory Court at the West End was built as a court room but rarely used, and so has been turned into a chapel. Externally, after extensive cleaning, the cathedral appears more brilliantly white than it would have done even in 1710 (the London smog must have blackened the walls of the cathedral even in the thirty-five years it took to complete).[14]

In general, the cathedral has held up to demands of the last three centuries remarkably well. The lead on the roof and the dome has been replaced, but most of the timbers are original, and although the external stonework has been cleaned, only a small proportion of it has needed renewing. Wren's methods of waterproofing the iron within his stonework have proven remarkably effective. There is, however, one matter that has stretched the expertise of many of the Surveyors to the Fabric since Wren, and that is the settlement of the dome. Concern over its stability had grown to such an extent that on Christmas Eve 1924 the dean and chapter were served with a Dangerous Structure Notice. They had been quietly repairing cracks that had appeared in the piers, but a piece of stone had fallen from the upper levels of the interior and there was concern for the safety of visitors. The building was closed and the then Surveyor, Mervyn Macartney, oversaw a comprehensive programme of grouting and the insertion of a very large number of tie-bars in the piers and additional stainless-steel chains around the dome. Today, there is considerable debate over whether this was a gross overreaction, and whether perhaps the cracks were perfectly safe, first appearing soon after the completion of the building. Whatever the case, the cathedral today is very carefully monitored as a precaution, so that any new movement in the structure can be accurately determined. So far this monitoring has shown that it is no longer settling and that there is no further cause for concern.[15] In terms of building construction, St Paul's has proven remarkably successful and a fitting tribute to those who designed and built it.[16]

***

It is certainly true today that architects tend to be remembered while craftsmen are largely forgotten. Of those involved in the works, John Oliver had asked in his will to be buried under the dome of St Paul's,[17] and Lawrence Spencer, the long time Clerk of Works, who died in 1719, was interred in the crypt alongside his wife and son.[18]

Wren himself was buried in the cathedral on 5 March 1723. The *Weekly Journal* recorded: 'Tuesday Evening the Body of Sir Christopher Wren Knt. lately deceased, the most famous Architect in all Europe, was carried from his house in St James Street Westminster in great funeral State and Solemnity, and was deposited in the great vault under the Dome of St Paul's Cathedral, the following plain inscription is engraven on the plate upon his Coffin. "Christopherus Wren, Eques Auratus, hujus Ecclesiae Architectus. obit. Feb 25 Anno Dom. 1723 Aetat 91."' The St Paul's archives record that his burial charges were met by the cathedral.[19]

Wren's tomb is actually not under the dome, as the quote above suggests. It is within a few metres of his daughter's tomb in the south-eastern part of the crypt, and remains a point of pilgrimage for tourists today. His memorial consists of an understated slab bearing the inscription: 'Here lieth Sir Christopher Wren Knight The Builder of this Cathedral Church of St. Paul &c Who dyed In the year of our Lord MDCCXXIII And of his age XCI'. It was his son who later added the words on a plaque on the wall above, which form one of the most famous – and certainly one of the most fitting – epitaphs ever written. Its motto could be applied not just to Wren, but to all those involved in the construction of this most remarkable building:[20]

LECTOR, SI MONUMENTUM REQUIRIS, CIRCUMSPICE

'Reader, if you seek a monument, look around you.'

EPILOGUE

Looking back at the seventeenth-century building world, it is striking how similar it is to the modern one. There are obvious differences in lifting technology and scaffolding, and steel and concrete have taken over as materials, but in other areas matters have changed comparatively little. It is clear that building contractors in Wren's time were businessmen like their modern counterparts, who often made a lot of money from their dealings; they worked on many projects at once, relying on employees to oversee individual jobs. There were the same concerns about corruption and profiteering as today, and similar careful systems of contracting and accounting in place to try to prevent them.

In Wren's office we also see the birth of the modern architectural firm, in which the head of the office retains overall control but relies on others for the execution. Wren's master craftsmen were also actively involved in the design process – in making drawings, producing models and in mocking up sections of the work for approval. All this was done under the watchful eye of the Surveyor, but there is no doubt that the design of the St Paul's was to some extent a collaborative effort.

One clear difference, however, is in the area of structural engineering. Wren may have been a renowned mathematician at the forefront of structural theory, but the ability to calculate forces and the strength of materials lay in the future. Wren still had to rely on the medieval practice of building models to test his ideas. This in no way diminishes the ingeniousness of his solution for the dome – indeed, his willingness to experiment is exactly what makes St Paul's such a startling piece of structural design. When faced with any problem, Wren appears to have considered carefully the various options before choosing the simplest and most economic solution. The result is an extraordinary building, which reflects the talents of all those who worked on it, and most particularly the mind of the man who is justifiably England's most famous architect.

FURTHER READING

There is a considerable literature on the cathedral for those who wish to explore the subject further. This book has concentrated on its construction. More information on other aspects and comprehensive bibliography can be found in *St Paul's: The Cathedral Church of London (604–2004)* edited by Derek Keene, Arthur Burns and Andrew Saint.

This book has very much relied on the original sources. A selection of the documents relating to the construction were transcribed and reprinted in the twenty volumes of the *Wren Society* (1923–43). It was these volumes and the manuscripts in the Bodleian that provided the source material for Jane Lang's *Rebuilding St Paul's after the Great Fire* (1956), now long out of print. The drawings for the cathedral in the St Paul's Collection have been reproduced in Kerry Downes's *Sir Christopher Wren: the Designs for St Paul's Cathedral* (1988) and the rest in Anthony Geraghty's *The Architectural Drawings of Sir Christopher Wren at All Souls College, Oxford: A Complete Catalogue* (2007) and all the drawings in the St Paul's collection are now available in an authoritative online catalogue written by Gordon Higgott. The latest ideas about the design are summarised in Higgott's 'The Revised Design for St Paul's Cathedral, 1685–90', *Burlington Magazine* CXLVI (August, 2004), pp. 534–47.

Wren is a fascinating character. The best short biography is probably still John Summerson's *Sir Christopher Wren* (1953). Lisa Jardine's *On a Grander Scale* (2002) and Adrian Tinniswood's *His Invention so Fertile* (2002) provide longer and highly readable accounts. The best study of his academic work remains Jim Bennett's *The mathematical science of Christopher Wren* (1982) and his writings and letters are reprinted in Lydia Soo's *Wren's 'Tracts' on Architecture and Other Writings* (1998). The most insightful account of Wren's architectural thinking is to be found in Anthony Geraghty's short book *The Sheldonian Theatre: Architecture and Learning in Seventeenth-Century Oxford* (2013).

Those searching for more information on the seventeenth-century building world should start with John Summerson's *Architecture in Britain 1530–1830* (1991) and Elizabeth McKeller's *The Birth of Modern London* (1999). James Ayres's, *Building the Georgian City* (1998) provides a beautifully illustrated introduction to Restoration and Early Georgian building techniques, while recent archaeological discoveries at St Paul's can be found in the two volumes John Schofield's *St Paul's Cathedral before Wren* (2011) and its sequel *St Paul's Cathedral; Archaeology and History* (2011). In writing this book, I found many new areas to research and I have written about many of these in various academic journals, which can be found online.

NOTES

Seventeenth- and early eighteenth-century England still used the Gregorian Calendar. This was a few days out of step with the Continent, and the New Year started in March. For reasons of clarity, I have changed dates so that the New Year falls in January rather than in March, but otherwise they remain as they appear in contemporary documents.

The references supplied here are strictly bibliographic, containing no asides or extra information, and are intended mostly for the use of scholars and researchers. I have not referenced the *New Dictionary of National Biography*, from which much of the additional biographical information has been taken. Where documents are reprinted in *The Wren Society*, I have generally given that reference rather than the original manuscript, since it will be easier for most people to access. Works cited in the Further Reading section above are given by author and date only.

Abbreviations

Biog. Dict.	Howard M. Colvin, *A Biographical Dictionary of British Architects, 1600–1840* (3rd edn 1995)
King's Works	Howard M. Colvin (ed.), *History of the King's Works* (1963–82), vol. V
GL	Documents formerly in the Guildhall Library, now in the London Metropolitan Archives. Original Guildhall Library manuscript references given.
Knoop & Jones	Douglas Knoop and G. P. Jones, *The London Mason in the Seventeenth Century* (1935)
Parentalia	Stephen Wren, *Parentalia or Memoirs of the Family of the Wrens* (1750)
StP	Derek Keene, Arthur Burns and Andrew Saint (eds), *St Paul's: The Cathedral Church of London 604–2004* (2004)
WS	*The Wren Society*, 20 vols (1923–43)

Chapter 1

1   R. Clutterbuck, *The History and Antiquities of the County of Hertford* (1815–27), I, 167–68.
2   GL CF 49.
3   David Crankshaw in *StP*, 62–64; Gordon Higgott in *StP*, 182–83.
4   *WS* XIII, 39–40; Higgott in *StP*, 183; Kerry Downes, *The Architecture of Wren* (1982), 6–7; William Dugdale, *The History of St Paul's Cathedral in London* (1716), 260.

Chapter 2

1   Andrew Saint, *Image of the Architect* (1983); *Biog. Dict.*, 29–45.
2   Mark Girouard, *Robert Smythson and the Elizabethan Country House* (1983), 20–21; *Biog. Dict.*; R. T. Gunther, *The Architecture of Roger Pratt* (1928); John Bold, *John Webb* (1989); Kerry Downes, *Hawksmoor* (1959).

3   Jardine (2002), 9.
4   J. W. P. Campbell, 'Sir Christopher Wren and Dr Robert Hooke' in P. Derham, *Loyal Dissent* (2016), 80–109; C. S. L. Davies 'The Youth and Education of Christopher Wren', English Historical Review (April 2008), 300–327
5   *Parentalia*, 181; Jardine (2002), 12–14, 25–36, 50–53.
6   Jardine (2002), 53–63, 72–86.
7   John Ward, *Lives of the Gresham Professors* (1740), 96.
8   J. A. Bennett, *The Mathematical Science of Christopher Wren* (1982).
9   Jardine (2002), 96–99, 122–25; Bennett (1982), 55–56 and *passim*.
10 Ward (1740), 1–38; Margery Purver, *The Royal Society* (1967).
11 Jardine (2002), 165–67.

12 Jardine (2002), 166–67, 180–83.
13 *WS* XIII, 39–40; Downes (1982), 6–7.
14 Jardine (2002), 70–71.
15 A. Geraghty, 'Wren's Preliminary Design for the Sheldonian Theatre', *Architectural History*, 45 (2002), 275–88.
16 *WS* XIII, 13.
17 Higgott in *StP*, 183.
18 *WS* XIII, 14–15.
19 *Parentalia*, 261–62; *WS* XIII, 40–42.
20 Report: *WS* XIII, 15–17; *Parentalia*, 271–78. Drawing: Higgott in *StP*, 184–86; All Souls Drawings Collection, AS II, 4, 6, 7; *WS* I, pls. vi–viii.
21 Evelyn, *Diary*, 27 August 1666; *WS* XIII, 20; Higgott in *StP*, 186.

Chapter 3

1 W. Bell, *The Great Fire of London* (1920), 22.
2 Ibid., 124–40.
3 S. Porter, *The Great Fire of London* (1996), 56, 71.
4 T. Reddaway, *The Rebuilding of London* (1940), 32–67.
5 Higgott in *StP*, 186.
6 *WS* XIII, 20–22.
7 Soo (1998), 56.
8 *WS* XIII, 22–23; GL 25,576.
9 *WS* XIII, 46.

Chapter 4

1 *WS* XIII, 49; *King's Works*, 15; Higgott in *StP*, 187; GL CF 54/5, xvii.
2 *WS* XVI, 193, 195, 199; possible earlier design in Higgott in *StP*, 186.
3 Gunther (1928), 213.
4 *Parentalia*, 282; GL CF 54/5, dated 16 December 1672; Hooke, *Diary*, 8 February 1672; Robinson and Adams (1935), 27.
5 Higgott in *StP*, 190.
6 *Parentalia*, 282.
7 Warrant reprinted in *Parentalia*, 281; claim in *Parentalia*, 283.
8 Higgott (2004), 534–39.
9 Clutterbuck (1815–27), I, 168.

Chapter 5

1 GL CF 54/5.
2 GL 25,471/16, 69, 72.
3 *WS* XIII, 34.
4 D. Woodward, *Men at Work* (1995), 209–49.
5 *WS* XV, xxxv, 155, 158, 163, 170.
6 GL 25,471/16A, 14.
7 GL 25,471/16A, 19.
8 GL 25,471/16, 88; *WS* XVI, 190; GL

25,471/16A, 8; *Parentalia*, 283.
9 GL 25,471/16A, 2, 8, 49, 57, 61, 68; *WS* XIII, 130; XIV, 5–9; XV, 79, 105; XVI, 55, 100–101, 103, 119, 129, 137, 151, 190–200.
10 GL 25,471/16A, 41; *Parentalia*, 284.
11 GL 25,471/16A, 51.
12 *Parentalia*, 284.
13 *Parentalia*, 284–85; GL 25,471/16A, 71.

Chapter 6

1 Duties in GL 25,622/1, 10–11; Spencer's life in Museum of London Archaeology Service, excavation, SAT00, 2000–2001.
2 GL 25,622/1, 5 August 1675, 10–11.
3 *WS* XIII, 33–34; GL 26 622/1, 11; *Biog. Dict.*, 714–15.
4 GL 25,471/27, 14 (*WS* XIV, 5).
5 Higgott (2004), 534–47.
6 *WS* XVI, 100.
7 GL 25,471/16, 47, 62.
8 *WS* XIII, 12; GL 25,471/16A, 36 (*WS* XVI, 195).
9 GL 25,471/16, 62.
10 GL 25,471/16, 65, 66, 68; *WS* XIII, 101.
11 GL 25,554; GL 25,643/1; GL CF 54/5; GL 25,471/16A, 73–80.
12 GL 25,471/16A, 47, 52, 55, 69.
13 G. Tindall, *The House by the Thames* (2007), 3–5, 58–59
14 Roger North, *The Life of Sir Dudley North* (1744), 198; GL 25,622/1, 9.
15 Gunther (1928), 20–22; Downes (1988), 49.
16 J. Walsh, 'Paper', in Jane Turner (ed.), *Dictionary of Art*, XXIV, 46, 49; A. Geraghty, 'Introducing Thomas Laine: Draughtsman to Sir Christopher Wren', *Architectural History*, 42 (1999), 240–45.
17 Downes (1988), 49.
18 H. Petrosky, *The Pencil* (1990); Geraghty (1999), 240–42.
19 C. Mitchell, *Inks* (1937).
20 Use of quill: information from Gordon Higgott. Supply: *WS* XIV, 77.
21 Downes (1988), 27–29; Geraghty (2007).
22 Downes (1988), 29.
23 *Parentalia*, 283.

Chapter 7

1 *Parentalia*, 292.
2 Ward (1740), 105; *Parentalia*, 292; Clutterbuck (1815–27), I, 168; C. H. Josten, *Elias Ashmole* (1966), IV, 1432; Andrew Clark, *The Life and Times of Anthony Wood* (1892), II, 317. Inscription on Wren's maul in the Museum of the United Grand Lodge of England, London.

3 *Parentalia*, 286.
4 M. Macartney, 'Some investigations into the soil in and around St Paul's Cathedral, and comparison with data in *Parentalia*', *Society of Antiquaries of London Proceedings* (1913–14), 218–28 .
5 H. Colvin in D. McKitterick, *The Making of the Wren Library* (1995), 41.
6 *Parentalia*, 287.
7 Vaughn Hart, *St Paul's Cathedral* (1995), 20.
8 *Parentalia*, 286.
9 *Parentalia*, 285–86; L. Soo, 'Reconstructing Antiquity', PhD dissertation, Princeton (1989).

Chapter 8
1 Summary sheet GL CF 49.
2 Letters Patent GL CF 64; Minutes GL 26,622/1.
3 Summary GL CF 49; in detail GL 25,555.
4 For coal in general, see J. Hatcher, *The History of the British Coal Industry*, I (1993); receipts GL 25,555, 25,475/2, 25,479, 25,480, 25,489, 25,478; ships 1687–1703, GL 25,473.
5 John Evelyn, *Fumifugium* (1661).
6 Reddaway (1940), 85; Hatcher (1993), 25, 502.
7 Reddaway (1940), 181–89.
8 *WS* XVI, 65, 85–87, 90–92, 94, 99.
9 Acquittance books GL 25,481; *WS* XVI, 77–78; *WS* XV, 35.
10 1 James, 19 May 1685 (GL 25,609).
11 7 William III, 22 November 1695, 1 Anne, 20 August 1702 (GL 25,609).
12 Summary accounts as above; Loans GL 25,610A indexed in GL 25,612.

Chapter 9
1 Soo (1998), 51–52; *Parentalia*, 275.
2 *WS* XV, xvi–xvii; *Parentalia*, 320.
3 *WS* V, 20.
4 *Biog. Dict.*, 641, 935–36; GL 25,471/19, 60–61 (*WS* XIII, 107).
5 *Biog. Dict.*, 641; Knoop & Jones, 35.
6 *Biog. Dict.*, 934–38.
7 22 and 23 Charles II c.11.
8 From Richard Grassby, 'Personal Wealth of the Business Community in Seventeenth-Century England', *Economic History Review*, 2 August 1970, 220–34, quoted in McKellar (1999), 69.
9 *Biog. Dict.*, 934–38; Clutterbuck (1815–27), I, 167; Knoop & Jones, 43–45.
10 *Biog. Dict.*, 576–77; Knoop & Jones, 4–6.
11 A.V. Grimstone, *Building Pembroke Chapel* (2009)
12 Knoop & Jones, 26, 80; *Biog. Dict.*, 754–55;

Higgott (2004), 537–38.
13 *WS* X, 44–53; Paul Jeffrey, *The City Churches of Sir Christopher Wren* (1996).
14 *WS* XVI, 166.
15 Knoop & Jones, 73–80.
16 Ayres (1998), 78; *WS* XV, xiv–xv.
17 Knoop & Jones, 56–62.
18 For saws, see Ayres (1998), 79–80; *WS* XIII, 93, 107, 116, 124; for lewises, see Ayres (1998), 74–76, *WS* XIV, 3.
19 Peter Rockwell, *The Art of Stoneworking* (1993), 89–106.

Chapter 10
1 H. J. Luow, 'Demarcation Disputes between English Carpenters and Joiners from the Sixteenth to the Eighteenth Century', *Construction History*, 5 (1989), 3–20; J. Campbell, 'The Carpentry Trade in the Seventeenth Cenury', *Georgian Group Journal*, XII (2002), 215–37.
2 Campbell (2002), 217–18.
3 John Fitchen, *Building Construction Before Mechanization* (1996), 85–113.
4 *WS* XIII, 148–50.
5 *WS* XIV, 40 and *passim*.
6 *WS* XIV, iv; X, 45–53; Campbell (2002) 218–22.
7 *WS* XIII, 75.
8 *WS* XIII, 53–54; X, 54.
9 *Biog. Dict.*, 1079.
10 *WS* XIV, iv; XV, 6, 84, 95; XVI, 103.

Chapter 11
1 GL 25,622/1, 5 August 1675, 10–11.
2 R. G. Albion, *Forests and Seapower* (1926); B. Latham, *Timber* (1957).
3 J. Campbell, 'Sir Christopher Wren, the Royal Society and the Development of Carpentry 1660–1710', PhD dissertation, Cambridge (1999), 68–75.
4 *WS* XV, xlv–xlvi.
5 *WS* XIV, 66; XVI, 27, 52, 63.
6 *WS* XV, 25.
7 *WS* XVI, 51–52, 54, 57–60, 73–74.
8 *WS* XV, xiv–xvi, xxiv–xxviii.
9 Letter Patent GL CF 65.
10 J. H. Bettey, 'The Supply of Stone for Rebuilding St Paul's Cathedral', *Archaeological Journal*, 128 (1971), 176–85.
11 GL 25,622/1, 17–18; GL 25,579/2; Bettey (1971), 177–78.
12 Bettey (1971), 184–85.
13 Ship size GL 25,494; repairs *WS* XVI, 67–68, 78.
14 *WS* XV, 144.

Chapter 12

1   *WS* XIII, 107–11.
2   *WS* XIII, 114; XIII, 160; XIV, 73–76.
3   *WS* XVI, 14.
4   *WS* XV, xlviii.
5   J. Campbell and A. Saint, 'The
    Manufacture and Dating of English
    Brickwork 1600–1720', *Architectural
    Journal*, 159 (2002), 170–93.
6   *WS* XV, xlviii; Reddaway (1940), 126–28.
7   *WS* XIII, 93.
8   *WS* XX, 237.
9   North (1744), 197–98.
10 Lang (1956), 120; *WS* XIII, 118.
11 Higgott (2004), 534–37.
12 Ibid., 543.
13 Ibid., 543–47.
14 *Biog. Dict.*, 437–78; Downes (1959); Kerry
    Downes, *Hawksmoor* (1969).
15 A. W. N. Pugin, *The True Principles of Pointed
    or Christian Architecture* (1841), 5.
16 Observation by Robert Bowles, in *StP*, 213.

Chapter 13

1   Lang (1956), 140–41.
2   *WS* XIV, 9.
3   Ibid., 9, 92, 101, 124, 134.
4   Ibid., 142.
5   H. Luow, 'The Origin of the Sash Window',
    Architectural History, 26 (1983), 49–72.
6   Ayres (1998), 190–96.
7   *WS* XIV, 139.
8   Ibid., 23, 88.
9   Ayres (1998), 194.
10 *WS* XIV, 146–47; XV, xix–xxiii.
11 *WS* XVI, 10–12.
12 Evelyn, *Diary*, 18 January and 1 March 1671;
    D. Esterly, *Grinling Gibbons* (1998), 16–66.
13 *WS* XV, xxii.
14 J. Newman in *StP*, 220–32; Esterly (1998),
    174–87.
15 *Parentalia*, 292.
16 *WS* XIII, pl. xxvii.
17 *WS* XVI, 23–24, 77–78, 81, 95.
18 Evelyn, *Diary*, 5 December 1697.

Chapter 14

1   D. Yeomans, *The Trussed Roof* (1992); and
    Campbell (1999).
2   Westminster Hall: J. Heyman, 'Westminster
    Hall Roof', *Proceedings of the Institution of
    Civil Engineers*, 37 (1967), 137–62; Trinity
    College, Cambridge: Royal Commission
    on the Historic Monuments of England,
    City of Cambridge, II, 225.

3   J. Campbell, 'Sir Christopher Wren
    and the Development of Structural
    Carpentry in the Seventeenth Century',
    Architectural Research Quarterly, 6 (1) (2002),
    49–66.
4   Campbell (2002); Yeomans (1992), 30–46.
5   Yeomans (1992), 148–61.
6   Yeomans (1992), 30–50; Campbell (1999),
    211–13.
7   Campbell (1999), 131, Appendix C49–58.
8   Campbell (1999), 188–89, Appendix
    C49–58.
9   Cecil Hewett, *English Cathedral and Monastic
    Carpentry* (1985).
10 *WS* XIV, 100.
11 *WS* XV, 167.
12 *WS* XVI, 72; Ayres (1998), 177–80.
13 *WS* XIII, 37–38; XVI, 31, 104–5.
14 *WS* XIII, 37; XVI, 30–31.

Chapter 15

1   *WS* XVI, 82–84.
2   Ibid., 85–86.
3   R. Mainstone, *Development in Structural Form*
    (2001), 118–20, 211–13; R. Mainstone,
    Hagia Sophia (1988).
4   G. and M. Fanelli, *Brunelleschi's Cupola*
    (2004).
5   *WS* XIV, pl. xlvi.
6   All Souls Drawings Collection, AS II, 43;
    Higgott, 'Wren's Designs for the Dome of
    St Paul's Cathedral', transcript of lecture
    to Soane Museum Study Group, 9
    October 2002, 5.
7   M. Whinney, 'Sir Christopher Wren's
    Visit to Paris', *Gazette des Beaux-Arts*
    (1958), 229–42; Soo (1998), 93–106.
8   A. Geraghty, 'Sir Christopher Wren and the
    Dome of St Paul's', *Annual Symposium of
    the Society of Architectural Historians of Great
    Britain* (2000); Higgott (2004), 534–47.
9   *WS* XVI, x; XV, 7, 35.
10 Mainstone (2001), 124–25.
11 *Parentalia*, 291.
12 Measurements from A. Poley, *St Paul's
    Cathedral* (1927); weight from Robert
    Bowles in *StP*.
13 Poley (1927), pls. ix–xi.
14 *WS* XV, xvi–xvii.
15 Fernando Marias, 'Piedra y ladrillo en la
    arquitectura española del siglo XVI',
    Chantiers de la Renaissance (1991).
16 *WS* XV, xvi–xvii.
17 *WS* XV, 106–7, 136, 155, 157–58; Soo (1998),
    67.

Chapter 16

1 Lisa Jardine, *The Curious Life of Robert Hooke* (2003), 15–19.
2 M. Cooper, 'Robert Hooke's Work as Surveyor for the City of London', *Notes & Records of the Royal Society*, 51 (1997), 161–72; 52 (1998), 25–38, 205–20.
3 Hooke, *Diary*, 9 September 1676 and *passim*; Jardine (2002) and (2003), *passim*.
4 T. Birch, *The History of the Royal Society* (1757; facsimile edn 1967), II, 461.
5 Birch (1757), II, 461.
6 J. Heyman, 'Hooke's cubico-parabolical conoid', *Notes & Records of the Royal Society*, 52 (1) (1998), 39–50; Hooke, *Diary*, 26 September 1675.
7 J. Hofman in Charles Gillispie, *Dictionary of Scientific Biography* (1970), II, 46–51.
8 Hooke, *Diary*, 5 June 1675.
9 Birch (1757), II, 48.
10 Heyman (1998), *passim*.
11 Higgott (2002), 6.
12 *WS* XIV, 124, 125, 134.

Chapter 17

1 *Parentalia*, 287–90.
2 Drawing in All Souls Drawings Collection, AS II, 37.
3 *WS* XIII, pl. xvii; XV, 62, 74, 132, 145, 152.
4 Jardine (2002), xi–xii, 424.
5 Bennett (1982), 41–42.
6 Jardine (2002), xi–xviii.
7 Ibid., 424.
8 Ward (1740), 105.
9 Poley (1927), pl. xi.
10 Palladio, *I quattro libri dell'architettura* (1570), I, pls. xxxi–xxxiii.
11 *WS* XV, 104, 122.
12 S. Price and H. Rogers, 'Stone Cantilevered Staircases', *The Structural Engineer* 83 (2) (2005), 29–36.
13 Information R. Bowles.

Chapter 18

1 GL 25,622 f. 20v; XVI, 75, 78, 97.
2 *WS* XV, xxxiii–xxxv.
3 J. Starkie Gardner , 'Introduction', 3, in *A New Booke of Drawings … by John Tijou* (facsimile of 1693 edn, 1896); J. Starkie Gardner, *English Ironwork of the XVIIth and XVIIIth centuries* (1972), 37.
4 *WS* XVI, 107, 108, 164.
5 *WS* XV, 117, 121, 145, 150.
6 *Parentalia*, 291.
7 *WS* XVI, 110, 149.

8 Ibid., 163–64.
9 Ibid., 163–65.
10 Ibid., 109–11, 150.
11 Ibid., 150.
12 Ibid., 151.
13 Ibid., 109–10.
14 Ibid., 111–12, 114, 159–63.
15 Ibid., 159; J. Campbell, 'The Finances of the Carpenter in England, 1660–1710', *L'edilizia prima della Rivoluzione industriale secc. XII–XVIII* (2005), 313–46.
16 *WS* XVI, 150–53.

Chapter 19

1 Ibid., 177.
2 GL 25,609.
3 *WS* XVI, 116–17.
4 Ibid., 123.
5 Ibid., 123–31.
6 Ibid., 126–37; *WS* XV, 225–26.
7 *King's Works*, V, 47–65.
8 *WS* XVIII, 181–85.
9 T. Sladen in *StP*, 233–56.
10 Ibid., 236.
11 *StP*, 220–32, 252–56, 258–68.
12 R. Bowdler and A. Saunders in *StP*, 269–92.
13 Information C. Faunch, Cathedral Archives.
14 Burman in *StP*, 258–68.
15 Stancliffe in *StP*, 292–303.
16 Saint in *StP*, 451–63.
17 *Biog. Dict.*, 715.
18 Museum of London Archaeology Service, excavation, SAT00, 2000–2001.
19 *WS* XVIII, 182.
20 Ibid., 182–83.

PHOTO CREDITS

Entries marked 'Pl.' refer to the colour plates section

The Warden and Fellows of All Souls College, Oxford: pp. 21 (AS II, 7), 28 (AS II.21), 29 (AS II.23), 33 (AS II.14), 58 (AS III.45), 132 (AS II.43), Pl. 4. The College's full collection of Wren's architectural drawings is available to view online via http://codrington.asc.ox.ac.uk/wren/

Dean and Chapter of St Paul's Cathedral: pp. 2, 92 (GL 25,579/1), 94 (both GL 25,579/1); United Grand Lodge of England: Pl. 2; United Grand Lodge of England and the Lodge of Antiquity: p. 80; National Portrait Gallery: Pl. 1; William Pryce: pp. 54, 113, 123, 136, 152, 153, 164, Pls 3, 5, 6, 8.